SASQUATCH

EVIDENCE OF AN ENIGMA (SECOND EDITION)

CARTER BUSCHARDT

BEYOND THE FRAY
Publishing

Copyright © 2020, 2021 by Carter Buschardt
Published by Beyond The Fray Publishing, a division of Beyond The Fray, LLC

All rights reserved.
No part of this book may be reproduced in any form or by any electronic or mechanical means, including information storage and retrieval systems, without written permission, except for the use of brief quotations in a book review.

ISBN-13: 978-1-954528-21-5

First edition, 2020 by Carter Buschardt
Second edition, 2021 by Beyond The Fray Publishing

Cover artwork & all interior artwork by Sybilla Irwin
Cover design by Disgruntled Dystopian Publications
All photos by Carter Buschardt

BEYOND THE FRAY
Publishing

DEDICATION

I would like to dedicate this book to my wife Sheila, who has allowed me to chase Sasquatch in the forest for days and weeks at a time. Her patience is a virtue. When she has had enough, I have promised her I will just sell all my equipment and grow a garden.

ACKNOWLEDGMENTS

I would like to thank the following people, in no particular order of importance, for their assistance and inspiration in my writing of this book.

Ron Morehead

Respected author of *Quantum Bigfoot, Voices in the Wilderness* and producer of the *Sierra Sounds* CD's. His thought-provoking insights and expansive thinking are a must have tool going forward as we seek answers for this enigma. **www.ronmorehead.com**

Sybilla Christine Irwin

Sybilla is an artist and researcher dedicated to helping witnesses who have come face to face with other worldly beings and creatures. I thank her for her kind and gentle soul and for contributing artwork for this book. Witnesses can contact her through her website at **www.sybillairwin.com**.

Matt Moneymaker / BFRO

My thanks to Matt for allowing access to the BFRO database for my published reports and general information to be used as part of this book.

FOREWORD

This book is written with all the passion, all the successes, and all the disappointments that go along with the search, and research, into the quest to prove the existence of Sasquatch, Forest People, or Bigfoot. Of course, depending on the event or incident, you could throw in fear, anger and serious frustration to top it all off. I have been an investigator for over ten years with BFRO as of the writing of this book. I have been investigating Sasquatch events several years before that, as well as several other "peripheral" cryptid events. But this book is all about Sasquatch/Bigfoot/Relic Hominids/Forest People or whatever name they go by in your world. For the most part they are all one in the same. Before I get going here, let me first say that every witness report in this book, every one actually happened, period. Each and every incident was real. Of course, names and exact locations have been changed, when needed, to protect the privacy and safety of the people, families, and property of those involved. But these are <u>ALL</u> real, down to earth people, who were lucky, or unfortunate enough, to have the event of a lifetime. They sought me out by referral or direct contact from my research page or through the BFRO site. None of them wanted anything from me other than to tell me their stories and get it off their collective chests. Some I interviewed in person, and some by long conversations on the phone. When you speak to someone after a cataclysmic event, you can just see or hear the sincerity. You know these witnesses have been moved to the core of their very being. Many uttered those very words, or very close to it. **Some were shattered emotionally and remain affected to this day.**

As I am quite fond of saying, these events happened to these people, and you cannot take that away from them, by virtue of ridicule, denial or shaming. All truth finds a voice eventually. If something so incredible happened to you, no matter **WHAT** it was, you would want to share it with someone, if for no other reason than your sanity perhaps, you want to get it off your chest.

I have had my personal sightings, and no one can take those events away from me. Go ahead and try. And when speaking to these witnesses you can tell almost from the start, that they are/were truly moved by the experience(s).

Some were believers already, and some were not. Most that were not believers, well, they are now! A rare few still question either the event and or the creature's existence. But they **know they saw something**.

Also, as several of my witnesses will attest, "I may not know **what** I saw, but I sure as hell know what I **didn't** see". Hopefully, right now someone is reading this book and saying to themselves, "Wow, that **HAS** to be what we saw", or words to that effect. By coming forward, in spite of peer pressure or public opinion, those in this book, and others not in this book, give those on the fence the courage to tell THEIR stories. For this book, the "proof" is believing in your fellow humans, and their willingness to put most everything on the line and tell their story and let the chips fall where they may. I applaud their courage. They wanted nothing from me, no publicity, no monetary gain. They just wanted someone to listen, without ridicule or commentary. For many, this was not possible with their friends, family, spouses, co-workers or in their close community. I thank them immensely.

Did I seek out or attract the fringe element or just plain crackpots, who wanted nothing more than to yank the chain of an otherwise very busy man? It is in the realm of a minute possibility, but very minute. There are a lot of hoaxers out there, but our/my interview process has a remarkable way of getting rid of them. Am I seeking to yank YOUR chain, the collective public, by writing a book based on phantom or overblown experiences? Less than even remotely likely. Those that know me, or of me, know that is not an option.

By the very fact I am an investigator of reported real events, it is my job and duty to ferret out the truth, and also to ferret out the liars, hoaxers and practical jokers. And there have been many of those. Some are pretty clever, and some are outright childish pranks. But they suck up my time, nonetheless. Comes with the territory.

Please remember as you read this book that you probably know someone who has seen a Sasquatch. Or, perhaps know someone who knows someone who has seen a Sasquatch. Or at least believes in the possibility of their existence. My witnesses over the years cross many personalities and occupations. Law enforcement, military, politicians, clergy, blue collar to CEO's. Doctors, lawyers, you name it, they are on the list and anyone else I missed is on there too. Some of my theories are in the book, as well as my personal beliefs. But I am fluid, and as I see, hear, and experience new things, I must keep an open mind. **My personal philosophy: If I don't know darn well nearly everything about a specific subject, then I must consider nearly anything that I come across to make an intelligent decision.** You cannot, and should not, discard an anomaly or possibility just because it is not in your current realm of knowledge, experience or belief system. That is an unproductive search for the truth. The opinions, theories, assumptions and educated guesses are all based on my personal experiences with witnesses, research in the field and any other available resources. There are potential abstract aspects to Sasquatch, as if trying to

FOREWORD

"prove" they exist isn't daunting enough. Throw in some abstract aspects and everything goes to hell. But I am on a road less travelled, and you may not agree or believe some of what you read, good enough. Any theory that is left of center will have tough footing, but I have to start somewhere. I chose to throw away 50 years of what **"THEY"** have told me, and actually learn by experiencing. It's clean and mostly uncomplicated.

And I can tell you why many witnesses, and critics of witnesses, will try to discount virtually everything thrown their way. If you were raised and taught that the world around you is just the way it appears and there is nothing "paranormal or extraterrestrial" in any way, shape or form that could alter the reality that you were taught, then you go about your happy life. Some folks go through life with blinders on, quite content to live and experience what is placed before them. All well and good. Nothing wrong with that. But those particular people will be hard pressed to deal with an issue outside of their comfort zone when it arises. Some of these people become the haters and critics when they experience things they can't explain.

I saw it, experienced it, but know it can't be, therefore I will reject it wholeheartedly with my last breath. If I see or hear a person who says they experienced something I know can't exist, I will make sure they know about it. I will make them miserable. And they do make some people miserable.

They are the haters and critics. We all deal with them daily in various forms. For those who have had an experience and want to search for another answer outside of the "accepted, usual and customary" teachings and writings, then please search, educate yourself, and reach out to other sources and people who are there to help. We/they are out there. My email is in this book. You may find that the very plausible alternative explanations may not fit into your comfort zone, that's fine. But at least you sought and found an answer, and if it doesn't fit into the world you have that gives you comfort, so be it. You will have that little bit of knowledge tucked away in a safe place in your mind. You can always access it later. As they say, you can put it in your pipe and smoke it another day.

Depending on your upbringing, education, and exposure to the real world in general, you will have a variety of reactions when you see, hear, or experience something that was out of your realm of belief just a few seconds before the event.

Remember the following:

Occam's razor (or **Ockham's razor**) is a principle from philosophy. Suppose there exists two explanations for an occurrence. In this case the one that requires the smallest number of assumptions is usually correct. Another way of saying it is that the more assumptions (explanations) you have to make, the more unlikely that occurrence is. It easily applies to science.

The above being said, there are events that defy application of this theory. If you are paying attention, you will know the time and place for application of this theory. But in general, at least try it for things that are well outside the accepted paradigm's you have for your life. You might be surprised.

And now, a word from and about your Author

As I mentioned in the introduction, I am an investigator with BFRO as of my writing of this book. I have led four public expeditions for BFRO, three in Missouri and one in Illinois. I have participated in and led night operations in many other public expeditions for BFRO. I cannot tell you how many private expeditions I have been on, but they are incredibly numerous. I have consulted on two of the Finding Bigfoot TV shows. I held a live Town Hall meeting in Independence, Mo. I have interviewed at least two hundred witnesses, and counting, over the years. I have had at **least** seventy reports published to the BFRO web site, and counting. Out of the published reports, I have met at least a third of them in person.

I trained as an investigator with MUFON before joining BFRO. I majored in Herpetology in college. I left college when I received a vicious bite from the music bug and was not able to recover. After that bite for or twenty years or so, I was a professional drummer in the 60s, 70s and part of the 80s. It was quite the wild ride and social education. If you name it, I did it, good, bad or otherwise. And I would not change a thing. I also had a four year run as an improv comic, sort of in the vein of "Whose Line is it Anyway".

Since an early age, say eight to nine years old, I had a serious interest in the "other worlds", the ones no one talked about then, and the ones that are somewhat ridiculed and scorned to this day. I just knew there was something else out there, some unknown thing or things that made the world a mysterious place. I made my mom send off for a free map of the solar system after I saved the required number of box tops, and when the map arrived, I was hooked.

But I wanted to know what was beyond the black void just beyond the one dimensional color print of the planets on a black background with no stars. There were stars at night when I went outside, yet the map of our solar system had no stars. Why? Multiply by at least several thousand that question and others. That has been my quest and mantra over the years.

We are all controlled by a bought and paid for media, government controlled disinformation, corporate controlled lobbyists with inexhaustible cash coming in from said corporations and others. Toss in the religious groups and evolution segments and there is enough garbage out there to keep everyone confused and many are happy to grab some of that as fact and carry on with their lives. If you are happy with what the media and others regurgitate and don't have the inquiring mind, there is absolutely nothing wrong with that. If you have a happy life, family, job, and all is good, why complicate things? You are happy and should stay that way.

WE ONLY KNOW WHAT "THEY" TELL US". I will

get into conspiracy stuff later in this book. As I mentioned earlier, I have had the pleasure to meet nearly a third of my witnesses whose reports have been published to the BFRO web site in person. I have met others whose events were not published for various reasons. Point is, it has given me incredible insight into their psyche, sincerity, veracity, and other insights as to their makeup. I have very rarely been disappointed after a meeting. There is a sense of trust and an open dialogue that continues to this day. I am a welcome visitor to their properties and anonymity is always assured. The ones I visit mostly are the ones with ongoing visitations and or habituations. I differentiate visitations from habituations in this way. My witnesses with Sasquatch visiting the property and or perhaps living on the property but they do not encourage or discourage the activity are visitations. They are comfortable with the comings and goings but do not offer any food or gifting or otherwise encourage any more activity than they have. They do not want to go to the "next level" just yet, or perhaps ever. They sometimes see them and hear them but do not seek out interaction. They are perfectly happy and fascinated with the live cryptid show. Going to the next level of habituation is a very big step. Sort of like, you like the new girlfriend/boyfriend, but do you want them moving in and all that goes with it? Habituation is pretty much an all in event. Habituation includes many of the following. Leaving food of all kinds at a specific spot on a regular basis to encourage a possible interaction. Maybe they are given an unlocked barn or outbuilding to use as a sleeping place in extreme weather.

Perhaps they gift you with some stacked rocks or twigs and you return the favor. Maybe they gift you with a small dead animal wrapped in grass as a token of appreciation. And so, the gifting begins. Habituations can be quite exhilarating but also exhausting. Once you get them used to food on a regular basis, especially foods they do not get in the wild, they can get pushy and a little upset at times when you slow down or stop the food offerings. It takes continuity and control to participate in a habituation and it may not be for everyone.

FOREWORD

Please read the next few pages carefully. This is where an open mind is a crucial next step in understanding.

I am also very open minded to things that are not totally physical in nature regarding Sasquatch events. **Anything**, my witnesses can tell me whatever they want. Remember my personal philosophy from before. I have experienced things that defy "logic". The logic "they" teach us. I cannot explain ALL of it, but I certainly will try. Or at least mention it. Quantum Physics, of course. There are many aspects of the Sasquatch that are reported to investigators, but those reports very rarely see the light of day for public consumption. But again, the events reported to us are the reality of the witness.

Even if some of the events are misidentifications, after a thorough review of the witness and the event, there are still a few that just leave you scratching your head. One has to at least give those few reports the time of day. If the witness has the courage to come forward to share an event, we at least should listen to them and give them respect for coming forward. **If we don't, then we are silencing a good number of rational sane people who have had an event that supersedes the mere sighting of a Sasquatch and goes to another level altogether.**

If your parents, spouse, siblings or very trusted friends were to tell you something that was off the charts "out there", would you discount them, call them crazy or some other description? If you know them to be sane, rational and truthful about anything and everything that they say or do, and one day they blurt out some incredible event with all the sincerity that they offer on a day to day basis regarding the day to day mundane events, do you suddenly discount them? If so, why?

Perhaps it doesn't fit into YOUR narrow or comfortable view of the world? Perhaps their "Star Trek" event is just too "WEIRD"?

Yes, perhaps there are aspects of Sasquatch behavior or attributes that we just don't get, as if the existence of these beings isn't enough to swallow already. Throw the other aspects in there and suddenly your spouse, siblings and trusted friends are suddenly nuts, when they were sane and rational the day before? Are "they" one of "those" people suddenly? Or is it <u>YOU</u> who are suddenly one of "those" people who suddenly distance yourself from a very good relationship because they saw or experienced something and told you about it? What would you say if they said they saw a UFO along with a group of your trusted friends? Same thing? That's different because even the government now says UFO's exist. So that event is ok, but others are not? What's the REAL difference? **You** are the difference.

My point here is that perhaps the problem is not the perception of the witness but the perception of the person hearing the information and their assessment of it. Remember, it could be you telling the story. If so, then what?

Say that out loud a few times, slowly. Inhale it and digest it. I can't discount everything I hear when it comes to the potential esoteric skillsets or attributes of the Sasquatch. But I do listen without critique. Who am I to scoff? We do end up discussing the possibility of what they are describing as perhaps being something else, (misidentification?), but when you DO get to that point of the conversation, it is hard to say it is anything else with a straight face. **It is the elephant in the room.** We HAVE to deal with it as investigators if we are being true to the ascribed title of investigator. I don't have to believe it, but I must consider it. Only thing that is fair and right. Some things just make sense, however abstract.

Yes, I am speaking of the fringe events of Sasquatch sightings and behavior. Not the road crossings or the standard blurry photos of the blobsquatch. At least 50% of all reported sightings are the road crossings and blurry creature in the woods.

And we need those to keep coming in. They are all very important and add to the database of behavior and geographic placement. But then......

FOREWORD

I am speaking of the cloaking, portals, orbs, different dimensions, mind speak, infra sound, zapping, speaking etc. Just as when the mainstream UFO phenomenon first emerged after the 1940s or so and those that reported them were deemed the lunatic fringe, or something else just as tasteless, we are at that point again. Since the government has finally acknowledged that UFO's do exist, those lunatic fringe torchbearers have some vindication. (A confirmed UFO does not mean they are piloted by a verified or specific life form, just that there does appear to be an intelligently controlled craft doing some physics defying maneuvers that we can't explain).

Now we have the Sasquatch emergence, and they go back thousands of years at a minimum as far as being mentioned historically by native and or indigenous peoples. So, they're here. As the usual and customary reports have trickled in and are accumulated into databases, we have a pretty well defined pattern as to disbursement geographically and some behaviors nationally and worldwide as well.

Those who believe through reading or outright experiencing them in the wild are the new "lunatic fringe". The UFO believers have been vindicated and passed the torch to the new "lunatic fringe".

I am proud to be a new member of this new group with realistically open minded research parameters. No dues need to be paid, other than the assault on your integrity and or sanity. For some few witnesses, or investigators that price is way too high. But, the closed minded should not have dominion over the mindset of others.

I mention this because now, we are getting the reports of "paranormal or otherworldly behavior or attributes" attributed to Sasquatch that we weren't hearing regularly before. Much as the UFO events started including abductions, impregnations, implants, etc. we now have the Sasquatch events starting to include inexplicable events that don't fit in our "accepted paradigm" of their behavior.

Doesn't mean that it is happening, but by virtue of hearing that option from reliable and trusted witnesses it doesn't mean it isn't happening either. We do hear more and more of it, and even if a trickle of it is true, we owe it to our witnesses and ourselves as humans to at least look into it. If YOU had an incredible experience, you would want to at least have someone listen to it without overt judgement. That is all I am asking here. Open minds. And that is what I offer.

If we can send a satellite 14 billion miles into space (Voyager) and receive radio transmissions back, put men on the moon, rovers on Mars (and likely humans as well, covertly of course), then that cannot be the limit of human achievement. There is a huge gap in there. This (Sasquatch research) SHOULD be a relatively easy fix.

Are you telling me that Government and Science cannot verify that a potential human relative is not alive and well in the forests and nether regions of our planet? This is what they are telling you and me. They sat on UFO info for decades and they are doing it to us again. They say we can't handle the truth as the human race. I say it is Government & Science that can't handle the truth. The dirty truth that they have been lying to us for centuries.

I am asking you to just consider the possibilities that what you are told isn't even worthy of consideration. You just never know.

I would also like to post this disclaimer. The opinions and or theories posted throughout this book are mine and mine alone. I am not speaking for BFRO or any one specific person within the organization, or anyone else for that matter. The reports posted and commented on are my reports and mine alone, except where noted. If anyone within BFRO shares my beliefs and or theories, I have no idea.

FOREWORD

Pretend you're here. Breathe it in

INTRODUCTION

This book is both for the casual reader who finds the subject of Sasquatch anything from interesting to incredibly fascinating.

And of course, for the novice to, the grizzled veteran researchers & investigators who may have everything from an open mind to a set of rigid concrete beliefs and anything in between.

INTRODUCTION

But, spend enough time in the deep forests and speaking to witnesses, and you will see & hear things from the rudimentary and obvious to the off the charts inexplicable. And I will be poking the bear and addressing the elephants in the room.

You may not believe me nor agree with me. Yet here I am. And here we go.

1
SCIENCE

As a profession, I respect "traditional science" in the amount of education & hard work I know it takes to become a "scientist". I truly do.
But as it relates to our endeavor to validate the existence of Sasquatch, "traditional science" is virtually non-existent. They scoff and exclude us at every turn. Not at all fair I say.

We, as researchers, may need to create our own science. It needs to be every bit as real and valid as the traditional science that discards us. We may even need to wander over to the quantum neighbors to borrow a cup of expansive thinking.

"The new statement is always hated by the old, and, to those dwelling in the old, comes like an abyss of skepticism" - Ralph Waldo Emerson

Science

WE ONLY KNOW WHAT "THEY" tell us.
Let me throw a few definitions (courtesy of the Collins Dictionary) of traditional science at you for starters. This definition is with a broad stroke, but you get the idea.

> *"The intellectual and practical activity encompassing the systematic study of the structure and behavior of the physical and natural world through observation and experiment."*
>
> *"**Science** is the study of the nature and behavior of **natural** things and the knowledge that we obtain about them".*

A **science** is a particular branch of science such as **physics, chemistry, anthropology or biology etc**.

Physics is the best example of a science which has developed strong, **abstract theories**.

...the science of microbiology.

OUR MAIN PROBLEM with relying on traditional or mainstream science is that it is entirely possible that they are simply ill equipped to handle the job of proving, or even considering the existence of the Sasquatch beings.

Perhaps we need to create our own science, complete with standards for criteria, and we answer to no one.

By the previous standards, which includes "abstract theories, as in physics" and "knowledge and study of the natural world based on facts learned through experiments and observations" we should have proven Sasquatch as an accepted life form by now. **The good old**

boys in traditional science have abstract theories as an accepted given by their peers. Our proof of Sasquatch is an "abstract theory" accepted by virtually no one. Me thinks I smell a double standard. Do as they say and not as they do. Hypocrisy at its finest. What is good for them is not at all good for us. By what standard do I measure **"proof"?** Before I get to that, let me say that **"traditional science",** is not our friend in any way, shape or form, as it relates to the topic of Sasquatch.

Most scientists, in my opinion, are pompous, arrogant, and seriously close minded as it relates to this field of study. They are too busy protecting the status quo, (no Sasquatch), protecting their cushy professorships, tenures and pensions. Here is a generic definition of a scientist: *"A person who is studying, or has expert knowledge, of one or more of the natural or physical sciences".* There are a rare few who venture past the prison walls of academia and closed minded thinking. And they are the risk takers and for them, we are grateful. But they are seriously outnumbered. Those few are strong of mind but weak in numbers. And they know who they are. I thank them. We the public thank them. But maybe we are using the wrong "scientists". Though sightings and interactions go back thousands of years at the least, traditional science, for the most part, refuses to acknowledge the existence point blank. Indigenous peoples, going back long before our current society, had written and drawn pictographs and petroglyphs of large creatures they either saw, or outright interacted with. This was before hoaxing and disinformation became the thing to do. They handed down their history from generation to generation. With the exception of a few countries or land masses, this is, and was, a worldwide occurrence. ***Most countries in the world have a word for a Sasquatch, Bigfoot, Yeti, Yowie and so on. Why? Because they existed and still exist today***. And the evidence or proof, continues to pile up today, tomorrow, and onward. They wrote about what they saw and lived. Remember that. Our ancestors may have been "primitive", but also realistic. So, why the denial, and probable hiding, of evidence proving the existence of Sasquatch? Other than what I outlined above, the status quo for so long has been denial. Since there would be a serious amount of egg on face to clean up and egos to soothe, they will just keep peddling disinformation or denial. Cleaner that way, and no scientist has to step outside the lines and make a mess of things. No upright Hominids, other than man, lived in North America. The "real why" would supposedly upset religious and scientific dogmas that have been pounded into our psyche for hundreds, if not thousands of years. And yes, there are of course, conspiracy theories. Some are probably very close to the truth, especially the political and monetary.

But some of the conspiracy theories are very compelling, and worthy of further investigation. Most of the evidence we have collected over the decades, including eyewitness accounts, would convict a person of a crime in many a court of law, if that circumstantial evidence was related to the crime and not Sasquatch. Yet, here we are. The "scientific community" is laughing at us from their ivory towers, but hopefully, not for long. Our facts and evidence are not facts and evidence in their eyes. And 'scientists' are only 'scientists' because they have a few letters by their names, and we do not. I can assure you that many of my investigator/researcher comrades are every bit the scientist as those with letters by their names, and then some.

One final note. Remember this if you get nothing else from this book. We/you, have been taught for generations that there are no relic hominids living in North America. No Bigfoots. No Sasquatch. Nothing. So, when and if you have an encounter, your first thought may well be, "I must be seeing things" or "it must have been a bear" or fill in the blanks with whatever excuse fits. You, and only you, know your reality. No one can dictate that through teaching, religion or intimidation. Your visual and emotional reactions to the world are yours, and yours alone. Enjoy, embrace, or reject them as you see fit. And, remember,

Our government and the "traditional scientific community" are not our friends. We only know what "they" tell us. We are all spoon fed our reality for our "protection". Question it all.

"No amount of evidence will ever convince an idiot". - Mark Twain

2

STRUCTURES

The Sasquatch, Bigfoot, Forest People, or whatever name you choose, are communicating with each other, and perhaps indirectly with us, right in front of our eyes. Most of you reading this book have seen or heard it in some form. You may just not know it yet.

From the very simple to the very complex, from the small to the towering, these creations are a road map to interspecies communication.

We humans are clever and smart. We put people on the Moon, build computers that dwarf the intelligence of the minds that built them. But we need to put those expansive minds to work learning about ALL the creatures we share the planet with. Even those that don't "exist".

We sometimes see things, but we don't really LOOK at them. There is a slight difference.

Structures & Knocks

. . .

(As symbols of language & communication skills)

Sasquatch have a language, just as we do. I have heard it in a variety of situations and variations. So have others who have been with me. If there is any doubt, then all one has to do is listen to the **Sierra Sounds** recordings made by **Ron Morehead and Al Berry** in the 1970s. They even make wood knocks, rock clacks, mimic virtually any animal on the planet, whistle, you name it, they can do it. If after listening to that series of vocals with an open mind, you cannot accept that there is possibly some living creature making those utterances, then this chapter, and probably this entire book, is a waste of your time. Read no further. But this chapter is all about structures and arches made by Sasquatch. They are the signs and signals made by them to communicate with other Sasquatch, and perhaps they are inadvertently communicating with us. And it is that "perhaps" I am going to discuss here. As we humans do when we want to speak without saying a word, we make signs, signals and writings to convey information to others. Traffic signs, billboards, written words, TV, etc. In the animal and even insect kingdom, there are all the sounds and symbols made by any and all creatures. Prehistoric man created glyphs, symbols and structures. You get my drift. It is in our very nature and DNA to reach out, communicate at all levels and temperaments to our fellow humans. Whether it is to communicate love to a loved one, or to tell the neighbor to keep their kids off your lawn, or to declare war, we communicate. Even a single digit salute to bad drivers is a form of communication. The photos I will be sharing here are from hundreds of outings, both private and public. The meanings of these structures are mostly speculative and philosophical as of the writing of this book. However, a very few symbols that seem to be reoccurring both in design and in areas where activity is seen or reported on a regular basis will be handled a bit differently. Those analogies will be based on my theories arrived at through a dozen years in the field, and commensuration with some of my fellow researchers and eyewitnesses over the years. Educated guesses through experience.

My theory is also based on my long-standing belief that Native Americans, indigenous peoples, and Sasquatch had at least a minimal mutual symbiotic relationship with each other. Scavenging and or outright sharing of hunting kills and potentially trading for crops. According to some theories, ancestors of Native Americans arrived in what is now North America at least 15,000 years ago, and potentially much earlier. If one takes into consideration that they may have come across the Bering Strait (Beringia) from Asia, as it is theorized that Gigantopithecus, (or whomever Sasquatch is related to), did as well, then the potential coexistence has deeper roots. I am not going to get into breaking down the minutia of that because that is for you to debate and or figure out.

I need a starting point for the theory and 15,000 years ago or so is as good as any. Native Americans have used symbols, signs, trail markers, etc. to communicate silently for thousands of years, and in my world, it is not a stretch to say that Sasquatch has been doing so just as long. Whether it is a learned and observed behavior or an ingrained human trait is part of the conundrum.

"Communication" has a **symbolic** nature and is an act of sharing one's ideas, emotions, attitudes and or perceptions with another person or group of persons. The use of words, written or spoken, gestures, signals, signs, or other modes of conveying messages are forms of communication."

Many simple structures are eerily similar to Native American symbols, and to discount that similarity as a coincidence is just plain ignorant. I don't believe in coincidences anyway. I am going to discuss one other caveat of the understanding and origin of structures before we get to the photo section.

Some of the structures found in the forests are very simple, and others are very complex. with the exception of a very few that COULD be chalked up to random acts of nature, it is more than obvious that what you are about to see are made by someone with opposable thumbs.That leaves 2 realistic choices, <u>Human or Sasquatch</u>, and we can't go there unless you address the odds of random trees, branches and or twigs falling naturally into a complex collection that happens to match symbolically similar structures known to be made by Native Americans or other indigenous peoples. Try this when you have a few moments to kill.

Take five chopsticks or branches and toss them in the air. How many tosses did it take to make a simple "X" or teepee? Got it on the first try? 25th? 50th? 1000th? $10,000^{th}$? Catch my drift? You will possibly die of old age trying before you ever see results, especially the very complex. Add to the equation the variety of species, length, diameter, whether cut or broken and living or obvious deadfall in the structures.

This is where the following data is important. With rare exception, most structures have at least 2 species of trees. The more complex has several. Take a 5 stick structure not counting the base tree. Ask yourself the following questions:

- How many different species are there in the structure?
- Are the branches cut or broken on the ends?
- Is there a corresponding tree(s) that match the species in the immediate area? Ten foot or less?
- If so, are there breaks and or missing branches in those trees that match exactly the broken components of the structure?
- If so, can you see how they might have fallen and arrived in the complex position?
- If not, then you have other questions to ask yourself.
- If they had to have travelled a distance of twenty feet or more from the base tree, and from a height of say twenty to eighty feet, how did they arrive in the exact position?
- Did they ricochet, bounce or slide? Were they windblown? Were they deadfall, and if so, do you see where they may have been laying prior to placement? And if they were deadfall, they were carried. The wind did not catch them just right and blow them up a tree.

So, for some of you, this might seem to be an over analyzation of data. But it is not. These forms of communication are vague, subtle and easily missed if you're not looking for them. And that is no accident. Many of you have walked right by them and either didn't see them or did see them and paid them no mind. So did I back in the day.

So, here we go. Keep an open mind. This is MY empirical data. Empirical data is information acquired by observation or experimentation. Sounds pretty "scientific" huh?

Crossed Line Symbols

The very simplest structure you will see more often than others is this one.

IN MANY NATIVE American tribes and or indigenous peoples, the X stands for man, or the male power or masculinity. They come in many sizes, and sometimes they form the basis of a far more complex structure. You will see them from just a few feet in height to some that are over 20 feet in height and or length of branches/trees.

If you see a structure that has a small circle above the X then it typically represents a woman and or the female power. It also represents nurturing and compassion.

A cross made up of a horizontal and vertical line is an indication of steadfastness. Steadfastness can also mean faith and devotion, but not necessarily in a biblical sense

A cross made up of a horizontal and vertical line is an indication of steadfastness. Steadfastness can also mean faith and devotion, but not necessarily in a biblical sense.

I will note that any X figure over two to three feet usually involves the use of a base tree because of the weight of trees in the X. Even the smaller X structures are usually made with a base tree, but on rare occasion they will be driven into the ground. This method is rarely permanent, because rain will soften the ground and wind will topple the trees.

That is why a base tree is used, and for **the most part** I will ignore the presence of the base tree as anything other than support. Yes, I know there are exceptions.

The definitions and theories of these three drawings are from the book: *Symbols of Native America* by Heike Owusu pages 14-15.

So, before we hit the photos, here is a Cliff Notes version of my belief and or theory into the messages conveyed with the structures. The same holds true for knocks, rock clacking, counting, howls and any other form of communication mentioned here.

WHAT IF A STRUCTURE(S) are the symbol for a spoken word in the Sasquatch language? Soak that in.

1. Sasquatch speak and have a language. See first paragraph of this chapter.
2. Structures are a form of inter species communication. Not rocket science. Anyone looking at one knows it is saying something.
3. Same holds true for howls, knocks, clacks, counting, etc. They are all messages to someone.
4. They may not be sophisticated like a "human" language, but they convey messages from rudimentary to complex.
5. If you have listened to the Sierra Sounds recordings with any type of open mind, then you realize these beings exist & communicate.
6. As with humans, if you can't speak it, then you make a sign or symbol.
7. I have heard the gibberish, "Chinaman's Chatter" and other random utterances in the woods. It is what it is. Language. I am not remotely alone in this experience. Sophisticated as "normal" spoken language? Perhaps not. Just because we don't understand it means nothing in the scheme of things.
8. I will refer to chattering, howls, whoops, knocks etc. as language as a shortcut word for "form of communication" simply for brevity as I write this. If you the reader are going to nitpick with semantics, don't.
9. Think of human sign language. Those born without speech or hearing have their own language and those of us that are not trained in the complexities of sign language have no idea what they are communicating to one another. But it is an obvious language.
10. With knocks, rock clacks, howls, whistles, etc., I firmly believe those are a language as well. They are not just sounds. It is entirely possible there are tones and or sub tones we cannot hear but they can. It is possible the spacing between knocks, the force or air moved by each

11. Do the number of pieces in a structure mean something? I think so. Three pieces, five or more, etc.? Yes. Height or length of pieces? Yes. Why use five, ten foot pieces to make a teepee or other structure, when it is probably easier to grab five twigs and create the same structure? As they say, perhaps size **does** matter, even to Sasquatch. Pun intended.
12. Does a teepee type structure indicate home to a solo individual or a clan/tribe? Why not? 2-5 or more pieces indicate number in the clan/tribe? Why not? Of course, a teepee/pyramidal structure would be the easiest to make and offers the strength needed for support and or longevity.

You get the idea. Open your mind to at least the possibility that there is something going on here besides random structures and arches in the forest. It is the perfect hidden language or form of communication. Like graffiti in the forest. We see it, sometimes stop to admire or wonder, then keep moving.

Again, what if this structure is a word, or a symbol for a word, or even an entire phrase in the Sasquatch vocabulary? Much like the Chinese polysyllabic characters or Egyptian hieroglyphs? Native American symbology? Or, a form thereof?

Photo 1 / **Yes, I am standing out on one of those limbs.**

Photo 2

In the large or tall X structures I am assuming that the base tree is needed for support and is not part of the structure meaning wise. Though the meaning of the X is a symbol of the male, it could also be seen as a warning to stay away or go no further. This would be especially true if blocking a path. It could be a dual meaning made by the dominant male saying stay away, this is our home or spot. It is not uncommon to find multiple structures in a relatively compact area, (twenty-five to fifty yards) and I usually refer to that area as their living room. I have seen five to six structures in a small area, it is obvious to me they spent/spend a good amount of time in that area. Sometimes there are smaller structures that are copies of a much larger one.

In my world, perhaps the smaller replicas of the larger structures are being made by the juveniles. Sort of a practice run or proving grounds. And even if the structures don't have the exact meaning as it relates to indigenous peoples, it is the most rudimentary of ways to communicate.

Photo 3

Throw a couple of logs against a tree and you have a shape and a meaning communicated with that shape. It is also a human trait to build and communicate. Either Sasquatch has actual human traits or is related to Man, or these are simply learned behavior and or mimicry.

Either way it is evidence of a highly intelligent creature. Is this a good example of the need for a third branch for support? X is the statement and middle is support?

Photo 4

Photo 4, was discovered in deep woods in southern Missouri. From ground level to horizontal log is eleven feet. There were species related downed trees from which that log could have come from in the immediate area. It was thoroughly searched, and I am certain that this was part of a downed tree. But it did not fall naturally into that position.

It was burned on the right two feet and was either a lightning strike or had been burned in a campfire when no axe was available. Seen that a few times before. None of that actually matters one bit because **it was placed and not a random fall, period**. For it to have fallen and land this way, it would almost certainly come in from the front AND in this horizontal position. The branches it is resting on are very small, about the circumference of my thumb. A log that size and weight falling, especially from that height, would have snapped them off without a doubt.

The branches it is resting on are very small, about the circumference of my thumb. Maybe a tad larger. A log that size and weight falling, especially from that height, would have snapped them off without a doubt. Mathematically possible but not remotely probable. This has all the earmarks of gentle placement. Hoax?

Odds of a person(s) dragging a ladder out to the middle of nowhere, and this WAS the middle of nowhere, to place a log eleven feet in the air for who knows who, and when, it was to be found also is a possible explanation but not probable. Hoaxers and jokers need instant gratification, as a general rule, when it comes to non-video hoaxing or joking.

Here is what put this structure WAY over the top for me. About one hundred yards to the rear of me standing there was a mostly abandoned post-civil war cemetery. Headstones dated from 1860s to 1890s. I have heard of and seen a few reports, of Sasquatch being seen in and around cemeteries. Even a rare few of them observing funerals in rural areas. I believe they bury their dead when possible and there are reports and tales of that being observed. I do not think it is a coincidence that this structure is a few hundred feet away from a cemetery. Remember this symbol is a sign of devotion or faith.

Photo 5 / Born Feb. 1880, Died June 1880. Short life of a child in the days of little or no medicine and sometimes very harsh conditions. Taken at the cemetery just up the trail from the structure below.

Now I cannot attribute faith and devotion as WE know it to the creature that erected this cross. It was more likely that seeing crosses at cemeteries and funerals is a direct result of putting observations of human behavior into an overt act. It is also entirely possible that the somber nature observed by Sasquatch was also noted by the builder of this cross and this could be a sign of respect, and MAYBE a touch of empathy. Maybe.

I would also like to note that this log was resting ONLY on the larger tree on the left. See photo 6 below. So, it is a true cross. The optical illusion of it perhaps resting on two trees is just the angle from which it was shot.

Photo 6 / from slightly different angle.

Photo 7

THE FOLLOWING structures you will see here are more complex, and as such, the meanings probably are as well. Conjecture, theory, experience and educated guessing are all I have to go on. Most of the structures were found with other investigators and or groups of people. They are MY witnesses. Since it is accepted among many investigators that the Sasquatch DO have a language that we have not yet deciphered, I am running with the theory that the simple and more complex structures are the "written word" or symbols that they are using to communicate with one another. Their language has no frame of reference for us yet. Nor do the symbols or structures. In my opinion, one cannot look at these and say they mean nothing other than random sticks falling into place.

And one more assessment of Native American/Indigenous people's symbols and a critique of trying to pin all structures on an interpretation or correlation to their symbols and drawings.

I have had to draw the line on myself several times. Basically, they don't work all the time. Once you get past the crossed line symbols, you get into V shapes which are really drawings. On a few of them it depends on which direction or side you are viewing them from. Here's an example.

< >

In many Native American tribes, the V pointing to the left signifies a respectful attitude, and or it indicates a person's ability to accept responsibility and respond. The V pointing to the right represents the power of grateful acceptance. It Also stands for the acceptance of truth. Well, if you WERE to see this structure coming down a trail from one direction it would mean one thing, and if you were to see the same symbol coming back from the opposite direction it would mean something else. This basis of interpretation doesn't work because these are drawings or symbols in <u>written</u> language, NOT symbology in our 3D world.

I have learned to use my assessment of a symbiotic relationship sparingly and have accepted that Sasquatch has learned certain things in the distant past and pretty much run with it and modified it to conform with their own traits.

A rational person seeing the above V's or arrows interprets them correctly as go left or go right. It means the same coming from either direction. *Go that way*. Probably means the same thing to a Sasquatch unless their language is far more complex and inclusive.

Photo 8 / Is this one a directional sign? That is the first thing that comes to mind to me as I will wager it is the same for you. If it is, then which of the two horizontal branches are indicating direction, top or bottom? Or both?

SASQUATCH

Photo 9 / Same photo as photo 8 with different angle. Note how similar this is to the V symbols we just discussed? See how easily you could misinterpret the meaning if you based your interpretation solely on meanings of Native American tribal symbols? Come from right side it means one thing, come from left side it means another. Common human logic says this is pointing to a specific direction or place. But what place and or what direction? And on which branch do you base your interpretation? Both or one over the other?

Photo 10 / Very similar structure but a much smaller version. It was within fifty to sixty yards of the one in photo's 6 & 7. It was also pointing in a different direction. Juveniles at play?

On the next page are two photos from the back side of this small structure. There is a lot going on in these next photos.

SASQUATCH

Photo 11 / shows one extra stick wedged in to perhaps offer more support.

Photo 12/ Arrow indicates older growth. See where the tree trunk on left has grown around the horizontal sticks. This creates a far more permanent marker and may or may not have been the intention. All of these structures were visible from the main road through this section of forest. They were not meant to be hidden. Not more than one hundred feet or so from the road, and they were on opposite sides of the road.

On photos 13 & 14, the structure resembles a Teepee. Does it symbolize a home for the Sasquatch or something else entirely?

Photo 13

Photo 14 / And yes, that is my apple core. Left a treat for the wildlife.

Photos 8-14 were all within fifty yards of each other. When I find this many structures in a relatively small area in relation to the size of the forest, I assume it is home or a favorite area for Sasquatch. Perhaps made by same clan or family. This area was their living room as I like to call it.

So, to interject here, this is a fabulous way to determine if you are thinking about trying to place a square peg into a round hole. In other words, trying too hard to explain something you can't explain. It is Occam's Razor (See Foreword for definition). You will see me refer to this a few times in this book.

Basically, the more you try to make something fit a possible preconceived notion of how you think it should be, the less likely that is the answer. Simple is better and is usually the answer. This can easily apply to all things Sasquatch.

Photo 15 / There are five branches "placed" in this structure. There are two living trees that have an integral part of keeping the loose branches in a specific pattern. There is a total of seven parts. You have multiple species all snapped or broken (not cut). You have multiple X's (male presence), if THAT is indeed the message. You have at least two directions represented here, if THAT is indeed the message. Do the five placed branches represent five members of a family or clan? Other options? What ARE they saying? This is a created structure, it did not fall randomly into this geometric pattern. The closest pine tree or pine stumps were dozens of yards away. You can see a vehicle on road in upper right of photo. So it was not far from road, about thirty yards or so. Not really hidden but not easy to see when driving by either.

The next four photos (16 - 19) show a complex structure in the way the branches are locked into place, not in the number of branches per se. Someone went to great trouble to assure this structure lasted awhile. The vertical forked branch was driven several inches into the ground. Think about that for a second.

Photo 16

Photo 17

Photo 18

Photo 19

The next three photos (20 - 22) I have titled *Hitching Post* for obvious reasons. On the two slender <u>outside</u> living saplings, each had a part of the fork broken off, so that the horizontal piece could be placed. See Arrows. In no way shape or form is this a random fall. Again, what are they saying or signifying? Portal? AND, these are **very** gentle placement.

Photo 20

Photo 21

Photo 22

Photo 23 / I have only seen one other of these. It is a fragile structure and placed out in the open, away from larger trees. I am guessing it was placed at this spot to be seen and to be mostly free from damage by other falling branches. Outer limb is snapped not cut.

SASQUATCH

I think you can now see my point. I can throw dozens more at you, but I feel I have made a case. I am going to finish off this chapter on structures by showing you one of the most complex I have found in the wild personally. It is very striking and complex in the manner in which it was constructed. It is almost art, in fact in my opinion it IS art. The structure was found in another area with at least four other structures. So, in an area of about fifty square yards there were five structures, all very different from one another, from simple to complex. Some had arches built into the structures, one had arches only.

Photo 24 / This one I named Papa Bear, Mama Bear & Baby Bear Arches. Just like the Three Bears. three different heights within eight feet.

CARTER BUSCHARDT

Photo 25 / This one was quite unique. The **right arrow** is the **arch** that was incorporated into the structure. It was pinned down at the other end by other parts of the structure. The **left arrow** points to the **main support** for the whole structure. It was driven well into the ground and was not easily moved. The **arrow at the top** shows the large **forked branch** that was snapped off on one end and jammed around the base tree.

Photo 26 / Shows back side and close up of locking and main support point. Pretty clever for a "primitive relative" huh?

SASQUATCH

Photo 27 / The Welcome Arch, greeted us as we emerged from the forest into the Sasquatch's living room. Note right arrow indicating the structure in the background (photos 23-25). This was an incredible area with at least five structures and gave off a very serene feeling.

Photo 28 / Three of my fellow researchers standing under the arch for a size comparison. The arrow on the lower left of photo indicates where the tip of the tree was driven into the ground at least a foot. I pulled it out, checked and immediately replaced it in a new hole just a few inches away.

As you can see in Photo 28 there is plenty of room for tall humans to walk through, and even taller forest dwellers. Many arches like this one start out as living saplings and are either bent over and pinned under a heavy object, such as a fallen log or large rock. Others, like this one, have the tip of the tree driven deep into the ground where it continues to grow. Some tips are wrapped around the large objects.

When you see a structure like this, it feels like a welcoming portal. It invites you to walk through, which we did. And yes, I can hear the critics saying heavy snowfall or another tree falling on a smaller tree will create this same effect. That does happen quite often, but the snow didn't drive this tree tip a foot underground, nor

SASQUATCH

was there a log pinning this one down. Just a fabulous, yet simple piece of work.

AND NOW FOR YOUR ENJOYMENT, a structure that was nearly sixteen feet long and had so much of a story going on. If only we knew even a molecule of their language and or thought process, we would have a chink in the armor.

And as it is, we are at least getting good glimpses at the evidence left behind. This one left us all speechless. Enjoy.

Photo 29

Photo 30

Nice close up of the suspended X's. They were supported by hooking one end of each X onto an outlying tree, which became part of the structure. Each end that was hooked onto the outlying tree was actually a branch that had either an L shaped end or a forked end that was broken off to form a perfect hook. This takes high intelligence and dexterity. This gives us only two choices as to the architect of this structure.

On the following pages will be close ups of the hooks. Simple, but ingenious.

Photo 31

I still think one has to consider the possibility that structures and arches may be symbols for a word or phrase in the Sasquatch language. They must be more than just ornamentation.

Photo 32

This is a closer view of the long version (Photo 31). It seems to me this was a double X when it was made. Maybe one stick deteriorated, or it was just made this way with a bit of ingenuity. Looks like double X to me. Arrow points to second X. There were no outlying trees from which to hang suspended X's on for the lower end, so the X's were just laid on the ground & main branch.

This structure had the feel of something regal, like royalty perhaps. It felt like it was made by, or for, someone of stature or importance. Hard to explain and you really just had to be there to understand the feeling.

Photo 33

    This entire area was about seventy to eighty square yards, give or take. It was bordered on one entire side by a large creek with a twenty-five foot drop off. The other three sides were bordered by moderate old growth woods that were easily traversable by one very long trail that had a lot of cutbacks. There at least five structures. This felt like home to someone. There was water, fish, shelter, ample game, and a bit of isolation. What are they saying with the structures? Were the Three Bear arches symbolizing a family or clan of three?

. . .

Was the single large arch a welcome mat or portal? Were they marking their territory? Whatever the structures are, they are intentional, intelligent and communicative. Food for thought.

Again, mostly supposition here, on the theory that many or most structures are conveying more than just eye candy in the form of simple to complex designs.

We have address numbers on our homes to tell other humans who lives there, and or how to find us. One to five numbers is common. Throw in the eight directional points of the compass. 814 NE. Main says a lot with very little. Throw in a zip code and you've said a lot more.

We have signs on our properties as warnings or general information. The larger or more verbose sign conveys more information. *Warning: Bad Dog. No Soliciting. Do Not Block Drive. Welcome to our Home.* We have those cute little stick figure decals on our vehicles that show the family breakdown. *Daddy, mommy, child, child, child.* We have billboards (structures). One structure can say as little or as much as space will allow.

Yes, I know; what am I smoking? Nothing actually. I am simply seeing things with a different set of eyes. Different point of view. They may have brute strength, but they are not brutes. They are far more intelligent than we give credit for. Structures mean something.

Photo 34 / The Welcome Arch behind me.

The next set of photos (35-37) are what I believe to be a Sasquatch communicating directly with me. As an expedition leader I do a lot of daylight scouting beforehand of the general area so that myself and everyone else knows where they're going at night. My method for scouting forest & fire trails is to write down the number of the trail as I enter that trail. I take notes and add it or eliminate it as the actual expedition nears. On this trail, after I got about one hundred yards in, I realized I forgot to write the number down, so I turned around at a fork after taking note of where I turned around and went to get the trail number. Trail numbers are only seen as you enter, not as you leave. It's my OCD. Anyway, I went back to where I turned around and this, (photo 35), was waiting for me.

Photo 35

This was not there when I turned around. It was two minutes tops for me to get the number, turn around and get back to the fork. Someone did not like my being there and let me know about it. So, in two minutes or less the tree was snapped and lying in the trail. I believe this was a message to me to stay out. Of course, that doesn't totally block the road as far as an SUV goes, but point made.

Photo 36 / There was no wind. No other tree fell & broke this off. It was healthy, moist and alive and you could see it was a fresh break. Fourteen inches around & the break was seven feet high..

Photo 37

This was an overt act letting me know they were not happy with my presence. I did not take it as threatening, as there are seriously threatening events that make this pale in comparison. Just a gentle reminder.

As my firm belief is that the structures found are communication between Sasquatch and or clans or families, this individual isolated incident was a communication to me to bug off. Now you see things like this snapped tree often, and if in the middle of a forest, off trail it could be interpreted as a directional sign. Go this way. Or, bug off. If blocking a road or trail, as this was, then the meaning is possibly quite different. There have been instances where a huge live, or dead tree, of great height, was pushed across a road with a massive snap and a howl or scream thrown in for good measure. No mistaking what that means. Many of my fellow researchers have see or experienced this and may probably gloss over this chapter as a been there done that moment.

But for the casual camper or hunters that go into the woods and see these things, perhaps it is another way to actually SEE the world around you and make you think. Think outside the box placed around you.

I could bore you with all sorts of structure photos, more than I have already perhaps. I could have added structures with dozens of pieces, twenty to thirty or more, no need; I think I made my point. Just consider, even for a nanosecond, that there is something going on right in front of us silly humans. Is it a form of communication, simple or complex? If you promise to consider it, it will be our little secret. But for the casual camper or hunters that go into the woods and see these things, perhaps it is another way to actually SEE the world around you and make you think. Think outside the box placed around you.

Property of Carter Buschardt &
Brian Woods.All rights Reserved.
©

3

KNOCK-KNOCK

Along with structures, there are other quite obvious methods of communication. Howls, knocks, whistles, whoops, howls, rock clacks, mimicry of other animals and sounds.

When in the forest, or wherever we may be, we have heard them. But we can't see the forest for the trees, so to speak.

They are more than interesting background sounds of the forest. Most will hear them, but rarely actually listen.

Wake up humans
(SASQUATCH CAN COUNT)

KNOCK -KNOCK. *Who's there?* Good question to ask even if you already know the answer. Another one of the most common forms of communication between Sasquatch is the knock. Though structures can be found in many deep & heavy woods, especially where Sasquatch have been reported, a knock is pretty much a long-distance Morse code call. Virtually any seasoned investigator has heard them at least once, and the casual campers and hunters have probably heard them and just don't know it. A knock to the casual visitor to the forests is probably just more background forest noise. You hear it but don't really <u>listen</u> to it. If you actually <u>listened</u> to it, you might question "what <u>was</u> that" or "who did <u>that?</u>" Otherwise it's just another sound or noise of the forest and nothing more.

A good knock can travel great distances depending on the atmospheric conditions, forest density, type of wood used both in the striking wood and the tree being struck. Throw in the amount of force used to strike while we're getting "technical". Major league hitter or pee wee T ball.

But the deeper question is what do they mean? And I will go after the simpler knocks first just as I did the simpler structures.

And I will put it out there that **Sasquatch can count.** A simple single, double or triple knock seem to be the most prevalent and they can be a very common way to say, "I'm here" or "we're here".

But to whom are they conveying the message to? Another Sasquatch or clan? Most likely. But if we humans hear it, is it actually meant for us, or are we just in the right place at the right time? Sometimes, if you hear a knock and return the call, you may get a response back. Does that Sasquatch actually know they are communicating with a human versus another Sasquatch?

We will assume that they are trying to communicate with each other, but every now and then a pesky human will jump on the party line and interrupt. So far, this is not rocket science, right? Fair enough and I'll try to bring it up a notch right here. Why do they choose a single knock over a triple knock for example? And why knock at all? One of the most simple and obvious answers to WHY they knock is to let someone know they are there. Duh. There's some rocket science for you. But what does a single knock infer? Here I am. Just one of me. What does a double knock infer? Me and my buddy Bob Sasquatch are here, just having a beer you know? There is a very short list of explanations.

My very simple theory, though slightly left of center, is that they can count. There is reasoning and calculation as to the number of knocks, be it one, two, three or however many knocks. Seasoned investigators know that sometimes when you pull into an area known for activity and get out of your vehicle, that a knock(s) will occur. Pretty much a notice to other Sasquatch that humans have entered the area. Heads up. (That's why you turn on your recorder before you leave the vehicle). Are they letting YOU know they are there, and they see you, and or are they telling other Sasquatch there are humans in the area? Probably both.

There is a reason they choose the number they do, be it one to three to however many knocks. Here is why I think they can count, and in some cases, it is not a random number for the sake of banging on a tree. Several of my habituation witnesses will report to me that when they go outside to work in the garden or do general chores, on occasion they will hear a knock or a rock clack. For them, since they know their surroundings and the patterns of behavior of the creature's they are sharing their property with, it means "we're here" ("I'm here"). A solo sound, whatever it may be, could have a dual meaning and be a count. One human outside dwelling.

After numerous months and even years of systematic "conversations" the witness and the Sasquatch simply know they are communicating. It is what it is and not rocket science. Happens often and is simple enough to be discounted by many. But here we go with a theory. <u>I believe they can count.</u>

One night, about five years ago, I had taken a group of six, including myself, out for night ops at a small lake. We had built a small fire and were listening to fish jumping in the water. There was a very irritating person who would not shut up, and was more interested in taking campfire selfies, and generally being a nuisance. I decided to distance myself from the aggravation, grabbed my radio and walked away from the group. After I got about 100 feet away there was a really good knock. Cool. Then when I got another fifty feet or so away, there were 5 more knocks, three knocks then two and with the same spacing between the three & two. Hmmm.....

That's odd but ok, I'm listening. My partner with another radio chirped in and asked if I heard the knocks. I responded affirmatively and asked him to join me at my location. The wheels were turning at this point. As he approached, there were two very solid knocks and as he arrived at my position, there were four more knocks. Same volume and same pattern, with very similar spacing between the four knocks.

BOOM. It hit me. They were counting us pure and simple. The solo knock then five was a signal that one human left the group, which was me. When my partner left to join me, there were the two knocks indicating two humans left the group and now the large group numbered four. When we rejoined there were 2 sets of three knocks each. Original group was complete once again. I was pretty sure of my assessment. Next event was another night op, this time with a large group of thirty or so, and my group was a group of eleven from the thirty attendees, walking single file late at night down a road that meandered through heavy forest.

As we do sometimes, my partner and I peeled off from the main group and lingered at least thirty to forty yards behind the main group. We do this to see if anything is trailing behind and keeping track of us. It does happen. So, we get to where we are keeping an even space between the group when bam-bam-bam......bam-bam-bam.......bam-bam-bam. Then bam-bam. Three groups of three knocks and one group of two knocks. Nine people in front group with nine knocks. Then two knocks for me and my partner.

There was a slightly longer pause between the last group of three and the two. In my world, not a coincidence. They were keeping track of us. Sasquatch can count.

When we returned to the group there were three groups of three knocks followed by the two knocks for us rejoining, but the spacing of the knocks between the last three and the two were in virtually the same cadence. We rejoined and the creatures confirmed by knocking.

One more example and I'll let it be. This is another one of those events that tops it off for me. The night mentioned in the previous paragraph with the group of eleven, we had an investigator who was using a wood block to do knocks. It's a very hollow sound but it does travel far. I had decided to take a few investigators, five to be exact, to show them the complex structures we had found the day before. When we got to the opening where the structures were, there were five knocks. One group of three then two. AND the knocks were identical to the hollow knocks from the night before, AND they guy who made them was one of our group of five that morning! No coincidence I assure you. First, it would take some searching, on short notice, to find two pieces of wood that would mimic that exact knock. If they even used wood. Think tongue clacking or popping. Cupped hand on a chest is another option as well. An extra set of vocal cords?

So, they saw us coming in that morning. Realized that the person who made the wood block knocks was there and made sure they made a sound that was eerily similar too whatever method or materials. When they made the welcoming knocks that morning, we sort of just stood there in silence. I reminded every one of the knocks from the night before and that the person making them was here, listening to a repeat performance. This was, to me anyway, an awesome example of advanced thought and communication!

No one disagreed, at least right there on the spot anyway. We went over all the previous night's activities after breakfast as we do on expeditions. We had the whole group of 30 there, sitting around the camp site having an open forum. After I threw my idea out there, another group mentioned that they had a similar experience with "counting" and the number of knocks matched the number in their group. No one separated from that group, but as they moved from area to area in the forest, there were knocks corresponding to the number in the group. I think there were six in that group.

So here we go. My theory only of course and you must at least *pretend* to think outside the box.

Perhaps all knocks are not counting, but perhaps when there is a larger group of humans, sometimes they are. Perhaps it depends on the perceived threat a human or group might be to a Sasquatch? If two people pull up and there is just a solo knock, what does it mean? Add any combination and scenario in there. **They are communicating with a very simple, to a complex organization of sounds.** Your dog, cat and other less "personalized" pets like herd animals, know the calls of their masters easily. They come, go or stay on your commands. A whoop or howl probably means a variety of things depending on pitch, timber, length and volume. It HAS to mean something.

Same with knocks, clacks, tongue clicks or chest beating. Any percussive sound made by Sasquatch has meaning to any member of the clan, tribe, etc. But what? We are missing something.

The amount of time it would take to sort it out would be monumental. One would have to be sitting in a very active area for a very long time and be present when everything started booming. You would have to make note of any and all activities witnessed as the sounds started, make more notes as to whether what you are seeing going on around you has anything to do with the sounds. Then calculate what you AREN'T seeing around you in the pitch-black forest, or perhaps a mile or more away in day or night conditions.

Does that knock or howl relate to an event you cannot see? As good a chance as any I'll wager.

You get it. But if you as a researcher, investigator, casual campers, hunter or reader of this book, just took a few moments when presented with sounds or signs that are out of place and or unusual and took some notes or even had a conversation, you might play a nice role in trying to piece things together. Virtually impossible? You bet. You have to start somewhere.

Structures, stacked rocks, rock clacking, knocks, howls, whoops, arches, chest beating or popping with a cupped hand, etc. They ALL mean something from one Sasquatch to another. Throw in that they can mimic virtually any animal and or sound they hear, then we are definitely on the outside looking in. They are giving us clues, lots of them. We just don't yet understand the language, yet. It can't be nothing. It has to mean something. Keep an open mind.

BFRO AND PRIVATE REPORTS

The reports in the next seven chapters are both published reports on the BFRO web site and private reports taken by myself from eyewitnesses who wanted to share the event, with no option of having the report traced back to them.

The BFRO published reports will have the report number included and will be verbatim (cut & pasted) as they were published. Any names or contact info and or locations will be removed for witness confidentiality. If the events were in public locations, those locations will remain. Report for any state can be found at **BFRO.net**.

The reports I include here are some of my favorites for a variety of reasons. But first and foremost is the event itself and the cooperation and veracity of the witnesses. I will include updates for the reports where there has been additional activity and or information given to me by the witnesses after the original publication in this chapter.

And if you want to have an experience like few others, I strongly suggest going on a BFRO sponsored expedition. They are led by experienced and knowl-

edgeable people and go to proven areas with past and current activity. **No guarantees of course, but at the least you'll learn things.**

BFRO Report Classification Breakdown

Class A: A clear sighting where the likelihood of misidentification can be ruled out to a greater degree

Class B: A long distance sighting with poor lighting which makes certainty of the creature unclear. Sounds such as knocks, howls, etc. with no clear supporting visual.

Class C: All second hand and third hand stories with little or no supporting documentation and or untraceable sources.

This is a general breakdown of the classification protocol. A definitive and thorough breakdown is available on **BFRO.NET Have we given the Sasquatch abstract powers or attributes because (science & government) cannot/will not explain their presence or existence? Or do they actually HAVE those powers and attributes, thus we can easily explain their entire existence away because those powers, attributes and beings simply cannot exist?**

And yes, you can read these, and other reports, on BFRO.net in their original form. They are actually in their original form here. So why are they even here then? Because I have maintained communication with many witnesses, either in person or by electronic means. I follow up after a few weeks or a few months or even years, to see how they have been affected further, or if at all. There is some great new info and insights here that are very fluid and change often. It is intriguing to see a transformation with witnesses. And myself as well. I'm still learning.

4
HOUSECAT

Photo courtesy of and copyright by Sybilla Irwin ©

Witness: Wendy P.
Location: Sangre de Cristo Mountains (Rocky Mountains), New Mexico.
Year: 2009
Report: Private

Wendy had been a "nature girl" all her life. She grew up outside the small town of La Cueva, in the Pecos National Historical Park which had an abundance of wildlife. As far back as she could remember she was always collecting insects and animals of all types. She had been the only child of two loving and happy parents, and they shared her zest for the outdoors. Camping, fishing and really anything in the wilderness, were nearly weekly events in her youth. And for some reason, as she grew older, she seemed particularly drawn to big cats; lions, tigers, cougars, bobcats and so forth. She found it fascinating that, much like dogs were related to wolves, that the ordinary house cat was related to big cats. And in the mountainous area she lived and played in, there were always reports of sightings of the big cats she was so attracted to.

When Wendy first contacted me, she was a forty-four-year old computer programmer living near her childhood home, which was about sixty miles southeast from Santa Fe. She was a self-described computer nerd and had the luxury of working from home two days a week and three at the office. This was ideal for her since she was not a people person. People often disappointed her, and animals did not.

When we first talked, she asked me far more questions than I did of her. She was quite reluctant to discuss her event at first because of all the ridicule from the "humans" that so often had disappointed her in the past. She was thoroughly interviewing me to be certain of my conviction and commitment to the Sasquatch enigma and to also be certain I was not going to turn on her with any disbelief. I assured her she was in good hands with an open minded "human", and she was not going to be ambushed. I have had my own events. I shared a few with her. So, who would I be to judge her? Problem solved.

Her report of the event.

Witness was riding her mountain bike along a fairly level mountain trail that would take her to her favorite area to look for big cat tracks. The trail she was on was actually a popular hiking trail that would take her to a game trail that was off the beaten path but still traversable with her bike to a certain point. Once the uphill climb from there got difficult, she would hide her bike and hike around to an area where she had luck before with visual sightings and had also found footprints of bobcat. And yes, she carried bear mace.

After getting off the main trail and going up the game trail about one hundred yards, she hid her bike and started up the game trail on foot. She noted an unusual odor as she hiked, "putrid and foul" as she put it. "Something died" she thought and just kept moving. She later noted that she had seen and smelled dead wildlife, and this was "a different odor". Once she got to an area where the smell was no longer discernible, she sat down on a rock to take a break.

After a ten minute break, she headed on up the trail. She heard a "ruckus" up ahead about twenty-five yards and off to her right in the woods. Sounded like a deer she thought, and after stopping for a few seconds, whatever it was had moved on, and she decided it was nothing of concern. Cats don't make that much noise and are usually stealthier.

She moved on up the trail to about the point where she had heard the movement and right there in the middle of the trail was what looked like a huge "puddle of urine". So fresh it was still "trickling down the trail" and was "orange in color, sort of like apple cider but clearer". It did have the distinct smell of urine and she was adamant about that.

So, since it was still "trickling" it was obviously very recent. A minute, maybe two at the very most she thought. First thought was a of course another hiker. At least she hoped it was a hiker. She stood there for a good ten minutes before she decided to move on. If it was a hiker they might end up hearing each other or run into one another. She moved on and not five minutes later she saw it twenty-five to thirty yards up the game trail and on a slight incline was a "reddish/grayish creature" she could only describe as a Sasquatch. It was seven to eight feet in height. It had its back to her but turned its head and upper body to the right and they locked eyes. As they were just "standing there and checking each other out" she heard a slight rustle in the brush to the right of the creature. It looked down at the brush and in a "smooth uninterrupted move" it reached down and appeared to grab something from the brush, turned around to the left and was again looking at the witness with a perfect side profile of the Sasquatch.

"It was clearly and without a doubt a female Sasquatch". "She had boobs"! Whatever she grabbed, if she did indeed grab something, was hidden from view at this frozen moment in time. The Sasquatch then looked ahead, which was into the brush to the left of the trail, looked back at the witness who was still standing on the trail. Then the Sasquatch started to take a step towards the brush, and as she did, it seemed to be "wrestling with something on the right side of her body" and she hesitated a bit.

During that hesitation is when the witness saw "the right hand and forearm of a juvenile Sasquatch, clear as day". It was "straight up in the air". She then saw the left arm of the juvenile come around the mother's neck from the right side and lock on to the left side of the mother's neck from the back. She was "carrying her baby piggy backed like all parents do"! This shifting all happened without the mother breaking eye contact. "We were both just still staring at each other". The mother Sasquatch then took a "short step over a rock on the left side of the trail, then a very long step and was gone" She saw and heard the first step, but nothing else. Whether the Sasquatch hid in the woods or moved on she has no idea. The witness just plopped herself down on a log and sat in silence for about thirty seconds and then began sobbing and heaving for what seemed like several minutes.

She later mentioned to me that she was not even frightened but probably more like shocked. She said she sat there for at least thirty more minutes and soaked in the event before deciding to move back towards her bike and the trek home. She found her bike and headed home.

My final report after interviewing her.

I spoke with the witness and this final report will include physical descriptions, movement, general assessment from the witness, as well as her and my final thoughts. We spoke in September of 2009 after her event of the same year.

As indicated previously, she assessed the height of the Sasquatch by using known heights of the trees and brush along a trail very well known by her and determined it was seven to eight feet in height. The Sasquatch was "almost an even blend of reddish and grayish hair of four to five inches in length. "Leathery dark brown skin" noted on face and side palm of her left hand when it was hanging by her side. Also noted same color on her "left boob" but it was minimal, as it was mostly obscured by "wispy hair" The skin color was described as something very close to Native American and Hispanic skin tones, but on the darker spectrum. They eyes were "black and penetrating" and she said she felt a "connection or some type of communication" and they seemed to be sized "somewhere between a golf and ping pong ball". She felt that the Sasquatch had an almost "sad or forlorn look on her face" and was neither afraid nor threatening. We were "checking each other out" and perhaps her sense of "connection" occured because they were both females and/or mothers. The Sasquatch was described as "as thick as Shaquille O'Neal with a pooched out belly". The arm was very long and hung well past her knee. The thumb placement was further down the hand than that of humans.

The juvenile was "darker then mom but I couldn't be more specific other than a dark brownish color". We were staring at each other while she was "fidgeting around with what I now know was the baby" so our eyes were locked when the "baby's arm appeared in the air on her opposite side". When it "reached around and grabbed around the mother's neck is when I finally realized what I was looking at" (baby), and saw it was darker". "Our eyes were locked until she turned and looked into the brush and forest on the left and disappeared". She estimated the length of the baby's arm at about eighteen inches or so. She thought out loud as we spoke, and she came up with a height for the juvenile to be about two and a half to three feet.

Since the baby was partially obscured by tree limbs, brush and hair it was only a guess. She was more certain of the arm length, however. The entire event lasted about fifteen to thirty-seconds or so.

As I have mentioned several times in this book, there are those raised a certain way that have a specific view of the world that is mostly rigid with very little wiggle room. This would be this witness up until the moment of the event. Being in the computer/tech field everything is ruled as black and white with finite boundaries and outcomes. She felt a "communication" of some type with the mother Sasquatch, be it real or perceived. She got the sense the stare down was protective in nature for all parties in the event. The eye contact was calming and unbroken until the mother walked off into the woods. She also had the sense that the mother was startled but also quite curious about this human that appeared on the same forest game trail at that exact moment in time.

The witness was frozen, literally, in shock. Never occurred to her to run. They just stood there and checked each other out, while the mother Sasquatch gathered up her unruly child and hit the road. That scenario plays itself out in shopping malls and play centers all over the world. The witness had heard of Sasquatch of course. But never saw or heard one before this event. She didn't recall ever thinking about them one way or the other until now. She may have seen a show or two. She is back at her self-described mundane but secure job doing something that she really loves. But her day to day life has moments of a thrill she will never forget. She has shared it with no one except her older son. Mostly because she is a shy introverted nerd who doesn't do people very well. I still get an email from her every now and then.

When we spoke, I didn't get a sense of embellishment or exaggeration. She wanted assurance I would not divulge her name or address, which I never do anyway. She just had to get it off her chest. She was very meticulous and precise regarding specific descriptions and surroundings. Her demeanor was similar to all the tech types I interview. She apologized for saying *boobs* to a perfect stranger, kind of funny actually. She is a down to earth, mother of a twenty something son living on his own.

She feels like this was supposed to happen, like someone tapping her on the shoulder to tell her to look around and check out what the world has to offer. She may be just listening to her inner voice. Who knows? She is grateful it happened and is looking forward to other events as she continues to search for big cats in the deserts and mountains of New Mexico.

Photo courtesy of and copyright by Sybilla Irwin ©

5
RATS

Witnesses: Ron & Kerry O.
Location: Malvern Arkansas
Year: 2014
Report: Private

Yes, rats, lots of them. Big wood rats in the wilds of Arkansas. That's where Kerry & Ronnie lived, in a nice three-bedroom farmhouse on forty-five very fertile acres in Malvern, surrounded by heavy woods on two sides. Plus, a big seventy-five by seventy-five-foot barn and loft. They swapped out corn and soybean crops every few years. And for some reason, they were seriously overrun with wood rats. They were everywhere and worse than ever before. They were nasty, mean and nearly eighteen inches long including the tail, and were eating their way through bushels of corn stored in the barn, leaving them losing money every day. They farmed, and they both worked part time jobs to pad the income. Didn't need to, just did it to retire early. But they got used to the extra funds after a while, and the loss of even a small amount of revenue on a nearly daily basis, well, not a good thing. And it was a small amount of money in the scheme of things. But of a more pressing issue was a potential infestation if they didn't nip it in the bud. The rats seemed especially drawn to a burn pile they had on the side of the property, almost even with the house. The home sat about a half-acre off the road that was in front of their house and the burn pile was to the right and was lined up just slightly in front of the front porch.

It was about thirty-five yards or so from the porch, and it was a small pile for some of the dead and rotting stalks and the normal waste generated by any home or farm. Ron's short-term solution for the rats was to go sit on the porch after dinner and before dusk and pick them off with an old .22 caliber rifle. It had a scope and was sighted in pretty well, though he told me he was a pretty good shot and didn't really need the scope. To assist him in shooting the rats once it got dark, was a very powerful hand-held spotlight. Kerry would join him out there every now and then. She held the light and he shot.

It was spring of 2014 when they first noted something was awry. As was his usual custom he would go out to the pile after a night of "shooting critters and varmints" and scoot any dead critters into the pile to be set ablaze at the next burn. They burned about once a week. Sometimes more depending on the carcasses and waste. And of course, some of the carcasses were pretty picked over as nature took its course but they burned whatever was left. Ron went out one morning after a good night of shooting to clean up the burn site. When he got there, he couldn't find the bodies of the rats; they were simply gone. He rummaged around and then he found a head., then another, and another. Five heads and no bodies. He knew he hit at least five the previous night and he saw them lying where he dropped them. *"What the hell,"* he thought.

The heads were torn off clean as far as he could tell. Definitely not cut. He later said it was a passing thought that they were bitten off but knowing the local predators and scavengers as he did, that scenario was not an option because they carry the kill off or eat them on the spot. The rats around there were in the half pound to up to a pound range in weight, and even at a half pound, the nights kill would be about two to three pounds; a good meal for just about anything known around there. He called for Kerry to come out and he showed her what he found. She looked and immediately asked where the bodies were and "was he pranking her". From the look on his face and overall demeanor, she could tell it wasn't a prank. He was more bewildered than concerned for this brief moment.

They looked around for a good ten to fifteen minutes and found no trace of the bodies. They were on a schedule and he had to get going to tend the farm and she had to get to town for her part time job. They were quite puzzled but decided to chalk it up to "some weirdness going on" and they tossed the heads into the burn pile for the next burnt offerings.

When they sat down for dinner that evening, they had both decided that sitting on the porch to see what was doing this was the best idea. It was probably happening after they went to bed, but no harm in trying anyway. They were running a bit behind normal schedule and they didn't hit the porch until about 9:30, nearly dark

Malvern time. Ron propped his feet up on the porch rail, grabbed his rifle, lit a cigarette and waited. Kerry brought a couple of wine coolers and grabbed the spotlight. They sat in silence.

It wasn't half a wine cooler later he got the first and then another. Kerry chided him for not letting her shine the light out there so she could "lend a hand" but no time to wait. Ron knew if he scuffed his boot on the porch the sound would make critters look their way, and the ambient light from the home would create eye shine and boom, easy pickings. After an hour or so they counted four rats knocked off. They went out and eyeballed each kill and then tossed them into the pile and decided they would burn tomorrow night, a few days earlier than usual since the corpses were piling up. No use adding disease to their plates. And there might be some more carnage.

The motion light went on around 1 AM and Ron jumped out of bed. He was half awake anyway as it was time for the nightly ritual of relieving himself. As he ran towards the window in the bedroom, he could hear some rustling outside but could not see anything yet. They slept with the windows open in spring for the fresh crisp air. He got to the window and saw the back yard all lit up and that was it. He could still hear the rustling and it was coming from the side or front of the house. Whatever it was, it was tearing through the brush and making a good racket.

Kerry woke up about this time, and watched Ron run to the living room and pull back the curtains. The racket continued a bit but was getting fainter, and whatever was out there was moving away. Ron then ran to the front door and hit the porch, grabbed his spotlight off the rail and shined it on the burn pile area. Nothing.

Kerry was now standing next to Ron on the porch. "Coulda been hogs I suppose," was all he said for the longest time. Kerry told me he was "pissed and kinda freaked out" and just sat in a chair staring out into the field for at least fifteen minutes. "Let's go back to bed and sort this out in the morning".

Ron was on the computer first thing in the morning. He decided it was hogs rooting around. As soon as he ate breakfast, he was out the door and headed over to the burn pile. He could see as he approached that it looked like it had been ransacked. Several very large and heavy charred tree trunks had been moved around. They were at least two hundred to three hundred pounds each and he could barely move them. Not hogs. On top of that all the rats were gone. Nowhere to be found, and this time no dismembered head. Not a trace they were ever there. This was getting "creepy & weird," and who the hell could move those trunks around? Certainly, not a known local predator or animal in general.

The fact the carcasses were gone was a sort of relief because they could easily have been carried off by any scavenger. That part made sense. The previous random beheadings did not make sense, which made the overall series of events just plain weird.

Based on the last few days of events, they decided to sit tight after dinner and stay inside and no shooting at the rats. Cut off the food source for whatever was out there and see if that would end the ordeal. A night of leftovers, a little TV and cruising the internet to possibly shed more light on their dilemma. They decided to lock the barn for good measure as well, just in case.

They both were awakened by the sound of "something or someone jacking with the barn door". Sounded like someone trying to pull on the handles and as they both bolted out of bed, the motion lights came on. As soon as they got to the window, they had a clear view of the back yard and the barn. They saw nothing and, as they were standing there, they heard a BOOM. Loud as hell and rattled the barn enough that there was "dust flying everywhere off the barn". More like an explosion than a boom, "like someone crashed a truck or something into the side of the barn," and from the view they had of the barn, front and left side, they knew whatever or whoever it was came from the rear or right side and they were still there. "This is enough of this bullshit" screamed Ron, and he grabbed a trusty shotgun and flashlight they kept in the bedroom, threw on some clothes and he was headed out the back door towards the barn.

When he got about halfway to the barn, he stopped to listen for any sound of whatever made that crash. It was eerily quiet, no bugs, frogs or any sound at all. Complete silence. He headed towards the side of the barn that was not visible from the bedroom and told whoever was out there he had a gun and they had better "get outta Dodge". He took a deep breath and swung around the corner of the barn with flashlight on and nothing. A clear view from the corner to the back of the barn and nothing but his well-manicured side yard. He walked to the back of the barn, looked around the corner, and still nothing. As he turns around and heads back to the front corner of the barn, he is shining his light up and down the side of the barn as he's walking and then he sees a big dent in the side of the barn about ten feet up. He is dumbfounded. The dent is about "the size of a soccer or volleyball" and the wood is splintered. He just stares at it for at least a minute, and then shines the light on the ground to see what could have made that dent. Nothing again. He wasn't really sure what he was looking for anyway. No woods nearby and nothing but corn on the side and rear of the barn. Now he's creeped out and calls for Kerry.

She calls back to him and says she's not coming out there. She is spooked and by now, so is he. He continues to shine the light around and walks back over to the dent. He takes the shotgun and holds it by the butt end and moves it up the side of the barn and places it at the bottom of the impression. ten-feet easy.

"I had no idea what or who could have done that" he later told me. There was no debris of any kind anywhere near that side of the barn. "I began to get scared and this feeling of unknown dread came over me" he stated, and "there I was, standing there starting to shake and quiver like a scared rabbit". He collected himself as best he could and decided to head back to the house. As he heads around the corner of the barn, he hears the most powerful scream he has ever heard in his life. "It bounced off my chest like a &*$%@# er" he told me. It was so loud he could not figure out where it came from other than it was in front of him somewhere. He paused for a second, pointing his shotgun at absolutely nothing, then realized Kerry was still in the house and he continued running towards her. She was already screaming and banging on the window.

As soon as he burst in the house, she was in the living room waiting for him. She was pointing at the window on the side of the house that was facing the burn pile. "Whatever that was came from over there," as she pointed to the burn pile. Ron headed to the front door with Kerry right behind him, adrenaline flowing. He grabbed the spotlight and handed Kerry the shotgun. He later told me his hands were shaking so bad he didn't want a gun in his hands. He shined the light at the pile and they both froze and stared at an unknown creature they had never seen, or even dreamed of.

They contacted me via email. They got my contact info from a friend of a friend who knew me quite well. My buddy had moved to Bentonville, Arkansas with his wife and we always stayed in touch. He told me they were in a total panic and needed to talk to someone. They had sent a very long email which was more a story than a report. They wrote everything down. I could have shortened it but left it as they sent it for the most part. Didn't want to lose the personality.

I called them and they relayed the entire week's events up to the sighting, so I was totally up to speed after about fifteen minutes.

He told me that when he shined the light at the burn pile, he was drawn to a lone tree that was to the right of the pile. There, squatted down at the base of the tree, was a dingy white creature sitting against the tree with its arms wrapped around its knees. It was holding a rat. There was some weeds and grass in front of the creature and from the calves down it was partially obscured. His first thought it was a person in a ghillie suit and maybe they were out there to steal stuff, but that thought went away quickly. He yelled at the creature to get off their property and then told Kerry to keep the gun pointed at the creature. He took another step or two, then the creature stood up, turned and ran into the woods to the right. It turned and looked their way one time and was then gone.

The description was as follows:

By the height of the trees and brush, the height was estimated at eight to nine feet tall. It had dingy white, or maybe very light grey hair, that looked like dreadlocks in several places. Could have been matted with clumps of debris. Hard to tell. Its eyes glowed a gold yellowish color, and they could not tell me if it was from the light hitting it or if it was emanating from the creature.

They could also see its teeth when they first saw it and it seemed to be smiling (grimacing)? The head was conical, and he described it looking like the old leather football helmets from way back, leathery and tough. They could not determine gender (weren't looking for that) and did note it was twice as wide as the tree it was standing by which they both estimated the creature was at least four feet wide. It was massive and built to "tear shit up", as he put it.

As we chatted, they told me they had been looking online to see what it may have been and they did run across Sasquatch but discounted it at first because no one around had ever mentioned seeing one, or even knew of someone who had encountered one. Heck, they weren't even sure if that Sasquatch stuff was true. I did mention Fouke, Arkansas, home of the Fouke Monster and the film Legend of Boggy Creek. They had heard of the movie, but thought it was just that, a movie. I mentioned that Fouke was just one hundred and twenty miles from them, and they inferred they had never been there. Up until a week or so ago they had never seen or heard anything that would have put them on alert, other than the missing corn. And they had locked up the barn, which they rarely did, in case someone was after more corn. I asked if there were any large footprints around the home or if there were any deer poaching corn from the fields. They couldn't tell me for sure, but were certain the deer helped themselves to corn, and most likely on the back side of the property, further away from the main house. As far as large (bare) footprints, they never noticed and certainly weren't looking but would be from here on out. They were totally blown away by the whole experience and were both quite shaken. It was not an area of interest to them one way or the other. I offered that those who lived in rural areas that grew large crops and or raised livestock could be easily prone to some loss of both. Never occurred to them. I also suggested that locking the barn was a good idea for them to prevent theft of damage to crops and property stored there, but they may have possibly frustrated a Sasquatch who had easy access to food and perhaps a little shelter from time to time.

The "beheading" of the rats I explained was a "usual and customary" rite of eating small prey. Easy to pop the head off so as not to have to deal with a pesky, snarling dinner as you chomped down. It is often reported. It could have also been a territorial event to let other Sasquatch and or creatures to stay away. As far as continuing the locked barn, tough shit they said. Barn stays locked.

I heard from them one more time about four months later and things were normal as far as they could tell. They had sniffed around town quietly and found a few folks who would talk about it. People knew but didn't talk. Small towns make fun of the oddballs. Never heard from them after that.

No more news was good news I suppose.

Note rat in hand.

6

BFRO REPORT #59520

Reprinted with Permission

Submitted by witness on Monday, May 28, 2018

Family describes the strange activity at their former rural home near Wesley

---

YEAR: 2002.
SEASON: Summer
MONTH: August
DATE: 2014
STATE: Arkansas
COUNTY: **Madison County**
LOCATION DETAILS: The Google maps directions are accurate.

The house is still there, but we moved two years after this incident and have not been back.

NEAREST TOWN: Wesley, Ar.

NEAREST ROAD: Highway 44 onto county road Madison

OBSERVED: We had things happen that we did not realize were possibly Bigfoot related.

1. There was an owl that would hoot every night. Louder than any owl I have ever heard in my life. We used to joke that it must be as big as a man. It was also slightly off sounding. Also, it called like this all year long. Not seasonally.

2. Our kids became afraid to sleep in their rooms. They said someone was watching them. They never saw anything, but said they just felt weird. So, they slept in our room with us. One night around 2 a.m. we were all woken up by a pounding on our house. Pounding so hard on the other side of the house that our bedroom windows were rattling. My husband yelled and it didn't let up at all. Just a rhythmic pounding.

Our gun case was in the room closest to the banging. My husband jerked that door open, grabbed his gun and ran outside with a flashlight. There was nothing there. He ran around the house and still didn't see anything. The next day we walked around the house looking for prints of some sort and there were no visible prints. The grass was very thick and lush at the time. Our nearest neighbors were over a mile away. This was about June 2002.

3. We had a momma goat that gave birth to twins. We found her and one baby dead by a pond about a mile from the house. Not much left of either except the hides. We thought it was coyotes or maybe a mountain lion, but even then, it seemed unlikely. More like they were carried there. No drag marks anywhere.

4. Our new neighbors and their children came over for dinner. My husband and our neighbor went to check Gates and cattle in a pickup. The kids were playing outside in the yard and the wife and I were talking in the living room with the door open so we could hear the kids. About 45 min before sunset, her 13 year-old son came up to

the house and told us he was scared. His mom asked why, and he said he heard something weird in the woods.

He was starting to tear up while he was telling us, but his mom said oh stop that, go play. And he did. I yelled at the kids and told them to come closer to the house and stood with the door open listening.

I thought I heard something off in the distance, but I thought maybe it was a bull and sounded odd because we lived down in a narrow valley. I stayed in the doorway watching the kids and chatting and heard the sound again and told the kids to come on in, because it was kind of creeping me out. I was feeling on alert but still wasn't exactly worried. My husband is a prankster and I thought he was trying to scare me. By now it's right at sunset and the woods about 100 yards from the house are too dark to see into. I heard the call again and I have never before or again heard a sound like that. By now the kids are freaked out, crying and telling me to come inside, my heart is pounding and I'm thinking that's not my husband....

The sound started low and slowly went high, I have no idea how long it went on but the thing that made that sound had to have MASSIVE lungs. It wasn't a monotone sound.

Almost like there were two sets of vocal cords sounding at the same time. A couple of very low sounds, almost like I could feel them in my chest more than I could hear them, and then it yelled again. It sounded like the call came from the other side of the creek about one hundred and fifty yards from the house, directly in front. I was more stunned than scared at this point, but my eyes were watering, and I did feel strangely sad suddenly, and I had backed all the way up to the door.

Right then the guys came back, from the opposite direction of the calls. We told them what we heard, and they listened but heard nothing, grabbed some flashlights and ran down to the creek and followed the creek about a quarter mile but didn't see anything. I didn't hear it again after that, but our kids never played outside close to dark after that either.

After that we had some stuff moved around or missing. A couple of dogs disappeared and one night it sounded like rhythmic tapping on the water pipes in the house in the middle of the night. My husband even crawled under the house to find out what was going on but saw nothing. The next day we saw the pin was pulled on the latch for the well house (by the creek) and the door was standing open. Just odd things like that. We didn't spend time outside at dusk or night after the August incident.

ALSO NOTICED: After the screaming incident we were positive this couldn't be anything else. We tried to rationalize everything away, but I truly believe this was a Sasquatch. I've heard foxes, bobcats, mountain lions, bulls, ECT and nothing has ever sounded close. I've heard male lions call and the power in the call is the same but the sound is not. Also, I had a pretty strange emotional reaction. I had that happen a couple other times out there. Once while I was carrying in groceries not long after the night, I heard the screaming. I left the rest of the groceries in the car, went inside and locked the doors.

I realized that my husband and I and also avoided looking out of any windows at night for quite a while before this incident. Strangely we never realized we were avoiding windows until after we moved. Even though all that time we were having to tell our kids there was nothing to be afraid of and that there was nothing looking in at them. This creeps me out to even think about now. It was almost like some sort of mind control or tranquilizing effect. It's very out of character for my husband and I to hide from anything. At the time it was like we didn't realize that we weren't spending time outside at dusk or dark. We just wanted to go inside.

Thinking back on it now it seems very odd like we were being manipulated. We didn't stay out and have bonfires or catch fireflies. No one was really afraid either though. It's hard to explain the feeling. Writing about it now, my heart is beating hard remembering the sound, but the night after the calling I don't remember being afraid. More just kind of numb feeling.

OTHER WITNESSES: For the calls: two adults and four children old enough to remember. For the pounding on the house: two adults and three children.

OTHER STORIES: After we had moved from the area we spoke with our neighbors and they had also moved due to someone beating on their house. It is an old two story stone house, foot thick walls. Her husband said he would never go back there.

People in the area have had full grown cattle attacked, dogs missing etc., but sporadically. Also, coyotes never came in this valley.

Down the road about a mile and a half you could hear them all over, but not around us. Neighbors up the valley raised sheep and lost a few, but never saw or heard a coyote. They had two Pyrenees watch dogs that stayed full time with the sheep, and we found them in our yard on a few occasions looking on guard like they had been following something. The sheep farm was a mile and a half from our house.

TIME AND CONDITIONS: It was a nice clear evening. Mid to late August about forty-five minutes till sunset until full dark. The other episodes were in the middle of the night.

ENVIRONMENT: The land lays in a twisting valley with a creek running through it. The valley is not much wider than the road in some areas but opens up where we lived. There is a house, small barn and paddock and a chicken house used to store hay in the area. About two miles to the South is a chicken composter that the landowner uses for culled chickens.

FOLLOW-UP investigation report by BFRO Investigator Carter Buschardt:

This witness and her family had been exposed to the ongoing activity for nearly the entire four years they lived at the home. The home they lived in was owned by the chicken plant her husband worked for and was part of the salary package. Free rent and a salary. They had eight children in total, and about half of them recall many or all of the incidents. I will address the incidents in the order she outlined.

The owl: As mentioned, it was "off sounding" and much louder than the others they heard. It almost always came from the same general area, which was a hollow near the home. At times, the owl would "sound like a normal owl, then evolve into almost a chatter or "gibberish". But it was almost always "way too loud" for a normal owl.

The kids afraid of their room: About six months or so, after moving in, is when the kids were "creeped" out about sleeping in their room at night. They felt like "someone was watching them" after dark. They almost always had cartoons or other kid type entertainment on at night, and the witness had surmised, after doing some research, that the "creature was attracted to the kids and their banter, and the TV on. When the banging on the wall started, they were out of there for good. After they abandoned the bedroom, they still used it as a playroom during the day, and up until bedtime.

It was after they abandoned that room when the banging started picking up and becoming more frequent, and only at night. The family kept their guns in a small room next to the kids playroom, and when the banging got really loud, hubby would head for the room, grab a gun, and the banging almost always stopped at that point.

Mama goat: The mama and her twins were very attached to the family and the house. Never strayed far at all.

When they found the mama and one baby, the hides were removed, not torn into or ravaged as a normal predator would do.

It was "skinned or peeled back". As stated, there were no drag marks or any blood trail, and they were pretty sure they were carried there.

The screaming incident: I will only add what was discovered during our conversation. Her account is pretty vivid and did not waiver much at all. The description of the yells were that it started as a low rumble type sound, which is why she thought it may have been a bull a few pastures over. But the sound "pounded her in the chest, and then the low rumbles turned into a higher pitched yell, but not a scream". In other words, the sound started out low then ended up higher before it stopped. It was described by her as a "lions roar" (the lower sound). I will address the "sadness or melancholy" feelings she had during this event later, as there are other similar "feelings or sensations".

Tapping on the water pipes: After hearing the tapping a few times, her husband crawled under the home to inspect the pipes and everything was in order. He then went out to the pump house to find the latch had been unlatched and the door was opened, but nothing was amiss. He tapped on the pipes to gauge where the pipes were being tapped on, and they figured out it was from the pump house, not from under the home. The sound traveled to the home.

CHICKEN COOP INCIDENT: This event was not in the original report, and this is where we delve into the theory of infra sound and melancholy.

She had gone out to check on the coop, as was normal before dark. On her way back, she was "knocked down by an unseen force or person". She fell forward and immediately rolled over to see nothing, or no one, there. She "felt" the push, but it was more an overall sensation of being "pushed" without the sensation of "hands on her". Almost "like a very strong gust of wind". We discussed infra sound, and other types of possible paranormal influences.

Let me say that this is a religious Christian family, with the "normal beliefs and practices" associated with their religion. Before they determined it was Sasquatch related, they had the family priest come out and bless the home and property to be certain there were no evil entities, and the priest said he had no inkling of anything of that nature. Also, of note, the witness began having migraine headaches shortly after moving in, and they ceased once they moved out. Home was tested for lead, carbon monoxide, and other possible contaminants. None were found.

There was a somewhat constant "suppressive atmosphere" the entire time they lived there. They had an unspoken "knowledge and agreement" that they would just not go near or look out windows after dark. Just a robotic existence. If you read her "Also noticed", she describes it perfectly. Many of the feelings and sensations they experienced are some of the side effects of infra sound. Confusion, lethargy, sadness or melancholy, discomfort, etc.

The mention of "two different vocals coming out at the same time" is not an unfamiliar description. When examining audio recordings of Sasquatch, there are many instances where there are "background sounds or calls" during one vocal recording. It could be two creatures calling simultaneously or just one with unique vocal attributes. Think Tibetan throat singing. Possibly two sounds from one source. I can hear the eye rolls. Stop it.

Regarding "things being moved around and missing" I will post this quote from her. "Just odd things, the shovel we used in the donkey pen, kids push toys we kept by the house would be down the hill by the creek, we had a wheelbarrow and a wagon for hauling feed, and they would be in a different place. The top part of the door to the barn was open most mornings even though we closed it every night."

The other peripheral instances of another family being driven from their home, missing or dead pets and animals, etc., are very consistent with reported Sasquatch activity.

This is an excellent witness, and her account is thorough, descriptive and reveals with great clarity the emotional effect this four year adventure had on the entire family.

*Oct. 17th: County was corrected to Madison County.

———

Final follow up with witness approximately 12/2018:

This is an intelligent well-read woman who did not limit her assessment of the events to her religion or upbringing. She researched many of the events and they nearly all pointed to Sasquatch activity.

After the chicken coop incident, when she was pushed down, she really began looking into all possibilities as to the source of the activities. She brought up infra sound before I had a chance to delve into it. They had even considered poltergeist activity as a potential source before calling the family priest. For her and the family, all options were on the table. If one reads very thoroughly all the events and activity, they are all classic Sasquatch related.

The things that bothered them the most and what ultimately forced them to move was her being pushed down by an unknown force or "someone" and the near zombie like behavior of her and her husband (and everyone really) as far as avoiding going outside after dark and avoiding even looking out the windows after dark.

Like she mentioned, it was totally out of character and it was like they just woke up one day and realized it was time to go. The location of both a sheep ranch and a chicken composter within 2 miles of their home was an incredible food source for predators and scavengers alike.

We also discussed the premise that Sasquatch are attracted to families, especially the women and children. With a large family of eight it is not a stretch to imagine high and overt interest by a family of Sasquatch.

Perhaps the creatures were banging on the house to voice frustration that the TV and kids were removed from the room. The entertainment was gone. Perhaps the Squatch liked cartoons too! The toys and tools left out that were moved around? Maybe they were "playing" too, after seeing the kids play. The toys and tools ending up down the hill by the creek got there via a circuitous route, meaning they would have had to make turns and dodge trees etc. in order to end up where they did. Not a likely scenario without help and guidance. Banging on the pipes in the wee hours? There was no mechanical situation where that would happen randomly, and only very late at night. Animals of both the witness and neighbors disappearing with no evidence of predator kill? (Yes, animals do wander off.) A neighbor being driven from THEIR home because of "weird" activity very similar to the witness's. The overall sense of dread, melancholy, etc. COULD have been infra sound (yes, among other things), which may have been a way to keep the family at a distance so they could be observed. Add it all up and it does smell of many reported events of Sasquatch activity reported by countless others. And yes, there are certainly other potential explanations. I am throwing coincidence out the window on this one though. An open mind is all I can ask.

This is my favorite Class B report out of most I have read or investigated. It has everything and more EXCEPT a visual sighting. Better than many typical Class A sightings. Excellent witnesses.

7

BFRO REPORT #63387

Reprinted with Permission

*Keep everything private, including exact location on Friday, September 20, 2019.

A family describes ongoing incidents near Meremac River outside Saint Clair

---

YEAR: 2019.
SEASON: Spring
MONTH: March
DATE: 8
STATE: Missouri.
COUNTY: Franklin County

LOCATION DETAILS: Withheld
NEAREST TOWN: Saint Clair Mo
NEAREST ROAD: Withheld.
OBSERVED: We bought our place five years ago on the Meremac River here in Franklin County Missouri. Things happen on a daily basis, like howls, tree knocks and something looming in our woods.

Our son used to travel home late at night on his electric bike two and half miles from town to home here. He stopped traveling at night (3 am) after something seven feet tall, white and hairy crossed a field next to the road and was gone. It terrified him so much he moved into town permanently and will not live out here.

Myself and my husband heard strange howl calls. I hear tree knocks on our back land and smell a horrible wet dog smell sometimes coming off the hill. I do not trail walk our land anymore nor do I go out at dark. I have chickens disappear from a locked coop and two peacocks killed inside a locked ten foot by ten foot cage. The two hundred acres down the road is where my son seen the one head towards.

As a Minister I was hesitant to write this but feel something is out here and in a group. I believe an investigation should be done. My guard dog refuses to be out in the back land area as if frightened of something. I won't even swim in our pool alone. I feel watched and a few times seen something tall in the woods but could not get the nerve to get closer. As we have found deer legs and parts that should not have been killed as we do not hunt our forest animals. Today I heard tree knocks again when I stepped out to feed the barn cats. Nope. I came back in it creeps me out. I almost want to sell our place but it's so beautiful out here. The bluff off the back land is a 100 foot bluff above the Meremac River. Lots of open spaced land in a deep hollow that is remote and thousands of acres around. Thank You for listening.

ALSO NOTICED: Always sounds or knocks on trees.
OTHER WITNESSES: Family.

STORIES: This happens a lot out here!!!!

TIME & CONDITIONS: 3am and my son had a headlamp light on that lit up a wide range as he is a cyclist and our land is lit up with outdoor lighting

ENVIRONMENT: Deep forest on the Meremac river.

FOLLOW-UP investigation report by BFRO Investigator Carter Buschardt: I had nearly two hours of conversation with witness and her son. Although he has moved from the property due to his encounter with the creature, he just happened to be visiting on the day I called. He was very forthcoming with the details of his event, as was the original witness. I will address the event(s) of her son as told in our conversation. I will then cover the lengthy ongoing events of the witness and her husband.

Here is a general timeline as provided by witness. Moved to the property in 2014. Started hearing "weird calls, knocks & noises almost immediately, but disregarded them until 2016. She intimated that since she was not familiar with those types of sounds, she just chalked them up to animals/forest sounds she wasn't familiar with yet. Witness and her son were on speaker phone together for the duration of initial interview.

Son was going home from work in 2018 around 3 AM as stated. He indicated he was going slower than usual because it had rained earlier, and the road was slick. The road at the point of the sighting was also downhill and an "S" curve, so he was not traveling fast at all for safety's sake. He was wearing a "very bright, almost blinding" headlamp. As he approached the first curve, which curved to the left, he saw this "mostly white creature tinged with some brown" on his left. It was "standing & stationary" in a field with a creek right behind it. "It was frickin' huge".

Distance was twenty to twenty-five yards at most. It was slightly ahead of him. As soon as the creature saw him (his light), it started "leisurely walking in the same general direction" he was going but veering off towards the creek. At this point he was just coasting and pretty much he and the creature were keeping the same distance between them. His gauge of height was the tree line and secondary growth. The entire event last "thirty to forty-five seconds". The creature was in no hurry and was heading for the creek and heavy woods on the other side of it. He stated, "it was not a bear and it was humanoid". As soon as he got home, he burst in the home and relayed the story. For clarity: when he said the creature "saw him" it just glanced slightly to its right once it saw his light and looked back quickly in the direction it was walking. No more physical features were observed.

Their dogs bring back "hind legs of deer and other various body parts". "Who would be killing and cutting up deer and just leaving them"? As stated, they do not hunt anything on their property and live in harmony with all wildlife.

Knocks: When she is alone, she will hear mostly a single loud knock, then another more distant or quieter knock. When she moves to another part of the property, she will hear another single knock.

Yesterday (Sept.20th, 2019) she found a "breath mark/smudge on a rear window of the home. Bottom of the window is eight feet off the ground.

She has the feeling of "being watched" and "I see movement in the woods". Her husband, who is Native American, has told her to "pay attention to the horizontal and vertical, as this is a way to determine what you are seeing". Man vs animal. This is his hunting logic.

They have had chickens disappear from a latched and locked chicken coop.

The two peacocks that were killed had their necks broken and were eaten and gutted on the spot.

The "horrible smelly wet dog odor" has been detected numerous times. Comes from the same general area of woods behind the home about twenty-five to fifty feet from the back of home.

This was an open and honest interview between the witness(s) and her son. In no way did I get the sense of embellishment. She went into much better detail as the interview proceeded, which I took as a sign of trust and she told me as much. In many instances, the fear of ridicule, especially in smaller rural areas with limited population, is very real. Of course, it can happen anywhere. This concern kept her from coming forward sooner. This investigator is glad they had the curiosity and courage to come forward.

The witness has a degree in Religion & Ministry. She is retired from active ministry. **Her grandfather was Cherokee, and her husband is Native American as mentioned. They live in harmony with all nature and do not hunt or allow hunting on their land.**

Yes, some of the events COULD be chalked up to predators or other natural acts. But as a whole and in the context of other reported events by witnesses deemed credible, this series of ongoing events is at the top of a short list for reports near the Meremac River in Missouri.

UPDATE:

The following is a discussion I had via phone about the events we originally discussed when I first got the report, and two other conversations I had with her husband about October 2019. Everything I am adding here is after the report was published in September 2019. It is my habit to follow up via phone with most witnesses a month or so after the initial report has been published, especially if there seems to be a regular and systematic presence or activity at a property. We can update reports already published on BFRO.net from time to time.

When I first chatted with her and her son on the initial interview, they were on speakerphone. It was a very lively and animated conversation. They were hearing a few things from each other they had not shared between them over the years regarding the activity. Since they were on speakerphone, I was hearing all the honesty and unbridled emotion between a mother and her son. It was innocent and revealing, and it left no doubt in my mind this was as sincere and real as it gets. Reminder: Her son had moved out after his sighting and popped in from time to time. We had scheduled the call for a Saturday, and he just happened to have popped in that very day. Totally unplanned. A nice gift for this investigator.

* Her son finally admitted that he had been seeing "a large human something looking in his bedroom" over the years. It had "large green glowing eyes" and it just stared at him. He estimated it to be at least nine feet tall. The bottom of the window was eight feet off the ground. This was the same window she had found the "breath mark/smudge on Sept. 20, 2019. When he mentioned this, she asked why he never told her. He didn't want her to think he was crazy, and he knew she was experiencing "weirdness" out there and he didn't want to freak the parents out any more than they were. He would just roll over, pull the covers over his head and go back to sleep.

I found it very interesting that the smudge marks were found very shortly after the son visited the home on his old bedroom window. I don't believe in coincidences. Same creature HE saw or the ones on the property?

* She told me that her husband worked an hour away from home, so that was a two hour round trip each weekday. He was up and off in the wee hours each day. With her son in school, and husband at work, she was out there alone five days a week. Much of the initial activity she was experiencing by herself, and it was a bit unnerving. Many times, the activity started when she went outside to tend the garden, feed the animals, clean the pool, etc. Her husband did not experience much initially since he was gone much of the time.

As she relayed what was happening to her, he too began experiencing some of the sounds as well as he payed a bit closer attention. I have spoken to him alone and he verifies that he has indeed heard more and more of the howls, knocks, screams etc.

* The peacocks that were killed were in a locked (latched) and covered pen. Peacocks can fly, hence the covered pen. Someone had to open the latch. Think opposable thumbs. They were gutted and guts were gone. Either eaten on the spot or taken off the property.

* With the dogs finding and dragging animal body parts up to the home, it is curious since they do not hunt or raise animals for food or sport. They live in harmony with nature and animals come and go at will. No one hunts their property. The deer hind quarter remains a puzzle to them. There are no signs of butchering. Sasquatch are well known for dragging deer down from behind and ripping the back legs off, rendering the animal incapacitated, probably leftovers.

* This final event is **very** intriguing. The witness and her husband often work in the yard together. Especially at the back of the home where it is closest to the woods.

Her husband has a nickname he calls her regularly around the house. Nothing complex, just a shortened version of her birth name. We all have pet names we call family members and significant others. Not a big deal.

One afternoon while she was alone, working in the back yard she heard quite clearly, **someone call her by her nickname.** She thought it came from the woods. As she was telling me this, she told me she was going to try to imitate the voice. I asked her to let me describe the voice instead, since I had heard, and used, a "Sasquatch" voice on a few occasions. Fine she said. I did my best impression and she exclaimed "Oh my God"! There was a good fifteen seconds of silence. She was floored. I nailed it. "That's it exactly"! OMG! Also, not a big deal. Once you have heard it, it is imbedded in your mind. Whether you have heard it in the wild, or on a recording, or however, it is not something you forget. Think *Sierra Sounds* if nothing else. Now she just stood there in silence, staring into the woods. Dead silent. No wind, movement, nothing. As she tried to continue her work, she couldn't, and she went inside to recover from the shock and just think. She also told me she thought she heard it a second time, on a different day, but wasn't sure, since it was a windy noisy day that time. She also said that if she ever thought any of the things she was hearing or seeing before the vocal event were imagined or other things, this put a lid on it. Done deal, there IS something out here!

This is a good witness and a good human. So is her family. Could she be mistaken? Possibly. Are the rest of her family mistaken? Theoretically possible but not probable. Four years ago, when they moved to the property Sasquatch events were not even remotely on the radar. Big city to rural wooded environment will do that to you, whether you have a belief system in place or not. They had no preconceived notion one way or the other. And look what happened to them. World turned upside down.

They want nothing from me. They want complete anonymity as to names being used, property address or location. Pretty much a witness protection existence. They wanted peace of mind and I hope I gave it to them. I will always give that to them. They wanted validation that they weren't crazy. As we spoke, she slowly warmed up to me and revealed more and more once she was comfortable that I was not going to judge. I could hear both the relief and emotion in her voice as we spoke. If she was a hoaxer or yanking my chain, she needs to be in Hollywood. She is wasting her time in the back woods of Missouri. And I have seen/heard some good hoaxers.

Now when you throw in an abstract concept such as a Sasquatch calling you by name, well a good majority of researchers/investigators will just take that report and stick it in the circular file. I don't and won't do that. If I/we don't give them the confidence to speak and be heard, then they will shut down and others after them will possibly be silenced, and we get nowhere.

And if you could have been on the other end of that phone when I mimicked the Sasquatch (in my very best Chinaman Chatter from "Voices in the Wilderness") and heard the emotion in her voice as the sound filtered through her mind, well, it was a Hallmark moment. And the silent pause. The sound of that was deafening, as they say. Moments like that are why I do what I do. Keep the open mind.

UPDATE 2021:

There are two events to share here. Both happened after the initial report was filed in 2019.

The witnesses called me rather excitedly one day in October 2020, and excitedly is an understatement. It was a Saturday afternoon. She called to tell me that her son and his buddy went fishing down at the river that Saturday afternoon. Since they are high on a bluff, they have to take a shortcut to get down to the river level which involves walking down a somewhat steep game trail. They do not go that way that often, but it beats the long way around, especially if you are really wanting to get started fishing.

As her son went down the trail first, he saw a small cave on the right, and almost immediately saw a Sasquatch bolt from the cave and run across a short clearing and disappear into the surrounding terrain. It literally ran right past him at a distance of no more than twenty to thirty feet. It was dark colored more black or dark brown and not really big at all. It was gone in a flash, probably a few seconds at most. Her son immediately ran back up the steep trail, which was wet and muddy and for most, it would be a nearly impossible feat, but fear can give one superpowers every now and then. I do not recall if his buddy actually saw it or not. But he was aware of the ongoing activity and certainly wasted no time hauling rear end out of there as well. They got back to the house, told his parents and she called me shortly thereafter. I went there the next day. Her son is the one who is mentioned in this report. He has seen them before. No misidentification on this one.

Follow up:

I got there Sunday around noon. We went straight to the cave. We went down the same way her son and buddy went. It was steep and slippery as advertised.

The cave was small and tucked in a corner and might be easy to miss if you did not check your surroundings. It was no more than about three to three and a half feet tall at the opening and about two and half to three feet wide. Pretty tight opening. When I got inside there was a high spot of no more than four feet right as you got in and then it tapered down and remained about three feet high throughout. It was no more than six feet deep and they very back of the cave was more like two and half to three feet high.

I cannot imagine a full grown big boy fitting in there with comfort. I am six foot two inches and was in a tight ball when I got in there. Possible of course if one needed a quick hideout.

What I found in the cave was intriguing. There were numerous children's trinkets. Small bottles of fingernail polish and model car paints, children's individual socks, no pairs of socks just solo mismatched socks, a few cheap plastic necklaces and some were broken. A few child sized toy trucks and cars, the kind a toddler might play with. One solid piece with no moving parts or choke hazards. A blue cuticle pen. I have a few photos at the end of the update. I hate to admit this as an "experienced investigator" but many of the photos I took did not make the transfer from my old phone. It happens I suppose. I beat myself up quite well over that.

The floor of the cave was mostly small chunky rocks and hard packed mud. No full or partial prints. No hair that I could find.

We discussed the trinkets and how they might have gotten in there. Since this spot is private property and accessible mostly if trespassing, the remote possibility of a child or two finding the cave and playing there is on the table but barely. Children of the age who would be playing with mostly toddler items simply would not be able or should NOT be able to get to that spot without adult supervision. If one were to access the river from a public spot or another private property then it would be possible to find this particular spot if out exploring. Just not a viable possibility but a very slight possibility. This cave is probably three feet or less below even a minor flood level, so to let very young kids go there alone would be unacceptable IMHO.

Another option which we discussed is that when the river does flood, all sorts of debris could wash into the cave. But to do so the debris would have to travel a circuitous route to end up in the cave around two turns and then straight back towards the river. And it would definitely have to be in the same bag of trash. A dubious possibility but being honest with oneself, it has to be a consideration, just like the previous consideration.

The other option would be a Sasquatch could raid trash cans, as is often reported, to scavenge for food. They see the shiny baubles and take them with them. Maybe an adult found them, or maybe a juvenile. If we impose a human child's mindset on a juvenile Sasquatch, then that would make sense. A juvenile would fit easily in that small cave, an adult, far less likely to fit.

Any three of these options are possible, some more than the others. I will leave it to you the reader to decide which scenario is more likely. It does fit the numerous activities reported by the witnesses on their property. If it looks like a duck and quacks like a duck, it may be a Sasquatch.

And.....on to Follow Up #2

A few weeks later they called me back with another event. Since I had walked the entire grounds of their property when I was out there for the cave event, I could follow their words and property as they described this event. Often before bed they go out back for a smoke or two before bedtime. It's a comfy spot that overlooks the back yard and woods. You can see the chicken coop, the pen where the peacocks were before they were killed, a small garden, etc.

As they were sitting there enjoying the dark and quiet they heard a heavy rustling coming through the woods. They grabbed a big spotlight they keep out there to view wildlife at night when the opportunity presents itself.

When they hit the area where they heard the noise, a big doe came crashing out of the woods, literally. She was obviously pregnant and she was running around in circles totally confused. She would head one way, then another, and then finally ran off into a different section of woods. She was either looking for or running away from something. They sat there for a short while longer and finished their smokes, and everything went back to the peaceful quiet they were enjoying. They decided to hit the bed and went back inside. Almost immediately they heard another commotion from the same area but considerably louder and longer.

They heard and saw three to five Sasquatch running around, quite agitated and chattering gibberish. They could see the outlines and humanoid shadows of various sizes as they were running pretty much all around the house. They seemed to be keeping just outside the ambient light from the house and exterior security lights they have as well. They detected numerous different voices and pitches and they were certain they were an entire clan or family that had been chasing the doe, and their spotlight had possibly chased her away from the property. They had lost an easy meal and were not happy. The body count of the Sasquatch was an estimate since it was impossible to keep track of all the shadows and shapes zipping by the windows. They used the different vocal tones and pitches to come up with an arbitrary number of beings circling the wagon so to speak.

After a couple of minutes all the excitement died off and it was quiet again. They headed off to bed. Yes, I am thinking the same thing. How does one even TRY to sleep after that? Well, let me answer that. You do not go RIGHT to sleep. As soon as they slipped under the covers they heard them again across the road from their house. The view from the front of their home is through heavy foliage and even during daylight the view is obstructed.

The neighbors across the street all have a ditch (small creek?), that is fed by a small natural spring, and it runs for a good stretch up and down the street. Now they could see very little but what they could hear was the big ticket item here. However many creatures were there were all drinking up that fresh spring water after the big chase of the doe. They were slurping, guzzling and pulling water up to their mouths with their hands and shoveling the water down as fast and as furious as they could. They could hear them gulping and swallowing and they could also hear mumbling. That ditch is around 100 feet or less from their front door and the sound was obvious and unmistakable and they were not remotely concerned with being quiet. They were thirsty as could be after the big chase and that clean fresh water was the antidote. From the time the doe crashed through the woods until the last drink of water was in the fifteen to twenty minute range. Sure beats a crappy movie on TV for entertainment huh?

Yes, they called a few weeks later with yet another event. And no, they are not attention seekers or crazy people. If you are at all familiar with habituation/visitation experiencers, this stuff just happens. It really does. I will admit it is hard to wrap your head around just seeing a Sasquatch in the first place. Seeing and or hearing them on a somewhat regular basis on your property is altogether another off the chart event when you hear someone discussing it. "Ain't no way no how as they say". But this does happen to the point that at times the interactions become just another event in a week or month of very busy people going about their very full lives.

This couple alternates between being amazed and sometimes

frightened. They are taking it as it comes and trying to just be neutral and roll with whatever happens. They remain undecided as to encouraging or discouraging the activity as of this writing.

Photos From Cave Adventure.

8

BFRO REPORT #55672

Reprinted with Permission

Submitted by witness on Wednesday, September 28, 2016.

Bow hunter describes close encounter at dusk from his tree stand near Grain Valley

---

YEAR: 2015
SEASON: Winter
MONTH: November
DATE: 25
STATE: Missouri.
COUNTY: Jackson.
LOCATION DETAILS: I-70 is about two miles south from my location

NEAREST TOWN: Grain Valley Nearest Road: Duncan
OBSERVED: I have been keeping this to myself since last year.

I have been a deer hunter for over thirty years and won't go back in the woods after what happened.

I'm going to bullet point this incident. I was deer hunting

Deer were running around the woods crazy that evening.

I had a small buck run past my stand, it was getting dark. 5:30ish.

He ran out into the middle of the field and stood there looking at the direction he came from for about fifteen minutes, then ran off.

Ten to fifteen minutes later I then heard this large something coming through the woods. Small trees breaking and leaves crunching.

I had no idea what it was, I had my back against the wide tree sixteen feet in the air, (the tree is wider than my back) and you can't see me or my stand from behind the tree.

It stopped right behind me, it is now dark, I could hear it breathing, it was eight yards behind me. I didn't move, it stood there for about five minutes then started sniffing the air like it was smelling for something, then it started to move slightly, it was dry out and leaves covered the ground so you can hear anything move.

Then two loud tree knocks, I then started to get a chill down my back, as I reached for my bow I heard two screams, I had my bow in hand and my shooting trigger was on my bow string and I WAS AT FULL DRAW. The screams vibrated the woods.

It stood there pacing behind my tree, left to right then stopped to smell the air again, it started to move West at a regular walk/pace.

I let off my bow, reached around the tree, clicked on my head lamp and about twelve yards from me was an eight feet, seven hundred to eight hundred pound, tall black figure, it grunted when my light came on and ran along the riverbank and back into the woods. I did not see a face. I saw the back of it.

I will say this, it was hunting that night, it was smelling for scent and chasing deer, looking for food.

At the time my bow was loaded with a one and half inch expandable broad/arrowhead, Yes I was at full draw not knowing what was going on, when my light was on and I drew my bow back again I was ready to shoot if it came back across the stream. I know the exact yards as I have hunted this location for around five years, I bow hunt, so I need to know the yards for arrow placement. This Sasquatch which what it was, was a massive animal. I don't know if it would harm anyone or persons but the power that I could see it its body was unbelievable. Yes, I was scared but I saw something that only a few people in the world have seen.

OTHER WITNESSES: no

OTHER STORIES: Only what I have looked up on the internet after my encounter. (Monkey Mountain)

TIME AND CONDITIONS: 6 pm. Clear sky and cold. Wooded environment. I could see the ground from my elevated position

---

FOLLOW-UP investigation report by BFRO Investigator Carter Buschardt:

I spoke with this witness for nearly an hour. Though we talked of course, a good bit about the incident, we also spoke of not letting this incident ruin his love of the outdoors and hunting. He has had time to relive the incident, and he has decided that he is going back out very soon to hunt and fish. I will go down the report line by line and add what was gathered during our conversation.

As stated, he was in his stand, sixteen feet up, back against a tree. Very wide tree and he and his stand cannot be seen from directly behind. 5:30-6pm in November so it is getting dark. He stated he sees pretty well at night. He was not using any lighting device at the time. Deer were plentiful and he saw several, including the small buck he mentioned. After the small buck entered the open field and looked/sniffed around at the direction he had come from, it left. He then heard something coming through the woods quite loudly, not being stealthy or covert at all. His initial thought was someone on a four-wheeler or a big buck, crashing through the woods from the same general direction the buck had come from. Thinking it was perhaps a trophy deer, he froze and just listened. As stated, it stopped about eight yards behind him, just past a small creek or riverbank.

As it stood there breathing, this is when he realized that it was something else, something quite huge. He could hear and almost feel it breathing. It was "huge, guttural, and you could hear the mass of the creature". Even though twenty-five feet or so away, he knew this was not an animal sound he was familiar with. It then began sniffing the air, (conjecture here) both looking for the direction of the deer and perhaps sensing the presence of the witness.

He was hunting scent free that night, meaning he was not masking his human scent. Being sixteen feet up and completely blocked by the tree, it is entirely likely the creature did not see him but may have sensed (smelled) his presence. It began moving around a bit and as he started to grab his bow, he heard two loud tree knocks. It did not knock on his tree, but one closer to the creek, or general area it was standing in. By this time, he was still reaching for the bow and had his hand on it, when two loud screams rang out. "Shook the entire woods and I physically felt it". In his words "it was like yelling at me hey.....hey...." By this time, it was almost directly behind the tree he was standing in, no more than a body length below him. It was pacing slightly and began sniffing the air once again. It was loud sniffing, drawing in huge amounts of air as though it was on to something. Nothing he had ever heard or "felt" (breathing) before. As it began to move off to the west a bit, (witness was facing south), he looked to the left at his 11 o'clock position, and hit his headlamp.

This is when he saw the creature, black, seven hundred to eight hundred pounds., from the back. "Big, powerful, muscular" and it went up the riverbank away from him and disappeared into the woods. It was approximately twelve yards away when he saw it. He did not see the face. He had an ever so slight side view for a split second, more like the back of the head and side where an ear would be. He did not see an ear. Hair was moving when he hit it with his headlamp, and it appeared dark brown or black.

Witness is an experienced outdoorsman and hunter, and as stated, thirty years in the woods, and is more than familiar with any and all wildlife in the area. He was truly physically and emotionally shaken by the event at the time, and vowed he was never going back into the woods again. He has since had time to reflect and decided that his love of nature and hunting has won out over any concerns he had over the event. For this investigator, to have a grown man, hunter and woodsman, admit he was frightened by "something" in the woods, takes a lot of courage, especially to a complete stranger. This, coupled with other known activity in the area, gives me no reason to doubt the veracity of this witness.

Numerous reports from this area, Monkey Mountain Park is close by. I wonder why they call it Monkey Mountain? Duh.

I have an ongoing habituation location not more than twenty-five miles from here.

I have personally had (and there are others besides mine) five other published reports from within a ten-mile radius of this location. It is a very active area.

You can go to BFRO.net and look up sightings by region in Missouri and hit Jackson County.

FOLLOW up with witness after publication of his report:

We have spoken and traded many emails since his event. The land he has hunted for at least ten years is private and no one but the owner and himself hunt the land. They are both very protective of the good hunting there and there is simply no one else allowed on the property. Owner does keep the gate locked. Property is used for grazing some cattle and haying.

In our first follow up conversation we discussed the possibility of me coming out there to meet the owner and walk the land and specifically the spot of the event. He indicated he had mentioned that to the owner, and it was a no go. He did not want anyone out there other than them, period. I get it and not a problem. I respect that.

He indicated he did not mention the event immediately to the owner, for fear of possible ridicule and or not being able to use the land. He sat on the event for nearly a year before he mentioned it to the owner. On subsequent visits to the property to hunt he noticed the owner had started packing a large caliber pistol on his belt. He had never seen him wearing a pistol. It was an old western style Colt .45. He knew he kept a large caliber rifle in his truck, and that was always there. Not unusual for rural landowners to pack a rifle in the truck. We do have big cats here, and coyote. He didn't think that much of it at the time. I didn't either.

He decided shortly after that visit with the owner of the land to tell him what he saw. They met again at the property prior to hunting and he noticed he was again wearing the pistol. Odd and out of character, since in the ten years or so he hunted the property the owner never packed a pistol.

He began to tell his story and as he got to the end of the event, he flat out just asked the owner if he had ever seen or heard anything of the kind he had just relayed. The owner pretty much cut him off and said, "We don't need to be discussing things like that around here" or words to that effect. And the subject was dropped. The owner was not rude or disrespectful, just business like and made it clear that topic wouldn't be discussed. Alrighty then.

My witness is quite certain the carrying of the pistol, and the edgy, jittery demeanor of the owner during the conversations pretty much told him this was not a news flash. They still remain friends, he still hunts the property, and as of this writing everything is back to normal out there, whatever that means. They just do not speak of the event.

I have probably investigated 10 reports at a minimum, of very intelligent hunters whose encounters were incredibly similar to this one. Carbon copies. Change the names and locations and the rest is verbatim. Very macho men and brave women who know the woods and animals that are there and or SHOULD be there. They are virtually fearless, safety minded and otherwise quite responsible folks.

But when a perfect stranger, a man of men and a woman of women tells you they will never ever set foot in the woods again, whether alone or not, day or night, and that they were in effect, scared shitless as they say, well, then you know that you are dealing with a sincerity that even those strong resolute people would be hard pressed to admit to under almost any circumstances, especially to a stranger.

To an experienced researcher or investigator, this type of event and the resulting follow up is probably something we have all been involved in.Nothing new right? For those reading this who are brand new to investigating or considering getting into it, these reports, and hundreds more you can read at the BFRO web site, can offer great insight as to the events going on all around us.

To the casual reader who may have no concept about Sasquatch one way or the other and is just interested in the subject as a way to enlighten themselves, this book will offer insights. Some trivial, some profound, and everything in between.

This witness rings true and I have no reason to doubt him. We remain in contact a few times a year. Good solid human being. As I mentioned earlier, he has overcome his initial fear of hunting those woods, yet he still has the belief that if you are in the wrong place at the wrong time with a Sasquatch then it's all over. I don't share that sentiment and am of the conviction if you mean no harm, none will come to you. All about intent.

9

BFRO REPORT #62930

Reprinted with Permission

Submitted by witness on Thursday, May 30, 2019.

Law enforcement officers' face-to-face encounter outside Dover

---

YEAR: 2003
SEASON: Summer.
MONTH: July
DATE: 11
STATE: Missouri
COUNTY: Lafayette County
LOCATION DETAILS: North on P highway from 24 highway. Make a right on Dover Bluff Road and immediate left onto Coal Mine Road.

NEAREST TOWN: Dover, Missouri
NEAREST ROAD: Coal Mine Road.
OBSERVED: In the year of 2002/2003 around 3:00 am during the summertime I was leaving my girlfriend's house in Dover, Missouri which is located on the Missouri River bluffs. At the time there were only two houses located in that area on Coal Mine Road.

One of the properties was owned by Kerr Orchard, which was in the midst of its apple season, and the other property was owned by the Dunkel family who raised livestock.

I was driving (Blue Ford Escort ZX2) south on Coal Mine Road from my girlfriend's house on the gravel road approaching the S-curve. As I rounded the first half of the S-curve, my headlights lit up a large, dark, sparkly/reflective object with yellow eye glow in the middle of the road. I began to slow down my car, and the reflective object hurried to the side of the road still on all fours.

As I got closer to the unknown object, initially I thought it was a black bear which is uncommon in this area. All of a sudden, the object stood up on two feet broadsided and froze as I continued to approach it in my car. At this time, I observed an unknown creature that was fully covered in extremely long (approximately eight to ten inches long), matted hair. The hair was black and gray and fully covered the creature except for the chest/shoulder area where the creature's skin appeared to be much lighter. I could see large, pectoral muscles in the creature, and at this time I knew the unknown creature was a male. The creature had very broad shoulders and extremely long arms that hung down beyond its kneecaps. I could not see the face or hands because of the long hair covering its body.

The creature appeared to be approximately eight feet tall and towered above my vehicle as I was about fifteen feet away from it still driving slowly down the gravel road. I would estimate him to be five hundred or more pounds and was solid muscle. When I passed him, I was so scared and down shifted my clutch to second almost killing my engine.

As I continued my drive home to Lexington, Missouri, I could not believe what I had encountered. The next day I told my mom/dad and brothers about what I saw.

Before the sighting I have driven home from that area in Dover, Missouri for five years and have never seen anything like it before. There is no question about what I saw that night. I know without a doubt I saw a male Bigfoot. In my opinion, the Bigfoot I observed appeared to be an unknown giant Ape that has not been identified by scientist yet.

ALSO NOTICED: Nothing unusual.

OTHER WITNESSES: No.

OTHER STORIES: Yes, at Baltimore Bend conservation area. My cousin (**name omitted**) had two separate encounters. Once mushroom hunting and another time squirrel hunting.

TIME AND CONDITIONS: 3:00-3:30 am. Summertime and very hot outside. No inclement weather conditions.

ENVIRONMENT: Apple orchard with apples on the trees and the other side of the gravel road had livestock in a fenced in field.

FOLLOW-UP investigation by BFRO Investigator Carter Buschardt:

I have had several informative conversations with the witness. As a law enforcement officer, both at the time of the sighting, and now, he is factual and methodical in his memory and reporting of the incident. At the time of the event, he was a deputy sheriff in Lafayette County, Mo. Location of event was in Dover Mo., which is sixty miles east of Kansas City Mo. To this day, he is still in law enforcement.

He had left his girlfriend's home at around 3AM. As he approached the first "S" curve, he saw a "creature of some type" in the middle of the road. It was down on all fours with "yellow glowing eyes". The yellow glowing eyes were just that: glowing. He felt that the hair was reflecting off his headlights and gave it a "sparkling" effect. After it moved to the side of the road it stood up. He slowed way down.

It was facing the side of his car with a full frontal view.

This was when he determined it was a male. As he passed it, it cocked its head slightly to the left while looking at him.

Physical characteristics are as follows: Long dirty/matted hair eight to the inches long with a mixture of grey and white, with some black as well. Clearly saw developed pectoral muscles. The hair was sparse on the chest and shoulder area and the skin was lighter, not tanned. At least eight feet tall and in the five hundred pound range. It towered well above his Ford Escort. Massive broad shoulders and very long fingers hanging below the knees.

When asked about the "glowing eyes" after it stood up, he stated that there was so much long matted hair that covered the face, that the eyes and face were completely hidden which gave him no facial features at all. Overall assessment of the creature was an "unknown giant ape" with a "massive body builder physique". It was not a bear, or any other known animal native to North America. He is adamant as to what he saw. And he has been an excellent observational witness.

I will mention the "Other Stories" and other anecdotal stories he told me, as they do give a back story to the general belief in that area that there is "something going on there" in that part of Missouri.

As an investigator, I have been to this area several times. Baltimore Bend Conservation area (1202 acres) has had several unconfirmed (not officially reported to BFRO) sightings and other activity. There was one report sent to BFRO, but it did not meet criteria for publication. As he and I were finishing our phone interview, his mother overheard our conversation and grabbed the phone and confirmed his story. She also confirmed the story of a "hairy wild man" that was rumored to live in an abandoned cave near the power plant in Lexington.

I also investigated a report (reported to BFRO) of two fishermen harassed by a "Sasquatch" during a nighttime fishing trip on the

Missouri River outside of Napolean, Mo, just a few miles west of Lexington.

The other "anecdotal" events reported were two sightings by his cousin at Baltimore Bend Conservation Area, calves missing from the cattle ranch when it was in operation. There were many reports of an abandoned cave (coal mine) that had "something screaming at you" if you tried to enter the cave. The old farmer that lived there still lives there and we are trying to get permission to enter the property as of this writing. I mention these peripheral events, as it speaks to the "common knowledge" of residents of the rural area that there have been things going on for many years. Several generations of families there all say the same thing.

Additional follow up information. (2019-2020)

I spoke with witness a few times over the past few months. The Kerr Orchards have sold to another entity and the name has changed. There is no connection to the new owners with any type of Sasquatch activity. The cattle ranch is no longer in operation as a commercial venture at this time.

Regarding the reported cave on private property, where something screamed at you when you tried to enter very, near his encounter, several attempts to get permission to get access to the land were unsuccessful. It was common knowledge in the area that these screams were going on several decades into the past. But the inability to either speak firsthand to the owners of the land, and or others that may have experienced those screams, leaves this portion of the report anecdotal at this time.

Of course, the screams they heard could have been big cats or perhaps bobcats of which we have both in Missouri. It does fit a pattern but simply cannot be verified.

The missing calves were verified over the years and the witness had spoken to the son of the former owner. They chalked it up to big cats, though no carcasses were ever found.

They just vanished. Either stolen or carted off. Again, the missing calves also fit a pattern but remain a mystery.

There were two items that remain intriguing to he and I, and we went over them in an email exchange. This was in regard to the eyes glowing and the sparkling effect of the hair. With the eyes, he was not aware of a difference between eye glow and eye shine at that time obviously, and he simply saw the yellow eye shine or eye glow between the clumps of hair hiding most of the face. (**Eye glow** is a self-generated light source from within and **eye shine** is reflected from an outside source, like headlights or flashlights for instance.) He could not address that with all the chaos of the moment but knew the eyes were glowing or reflecting from his headlights. So be it. The sparkling hair was quite intriguing to him (and myself), and he told me that it was "definitely not wet or even moist, completely dry and matted together" "It completely reflected off my headlights". "There is no question about the hair, **it is extremely reflective of light**". He further confirmed in an email in Jan. 2020, that the hair was **"reflecting silver only because his headlights lit the hair directly"**. "When I drove by it and saw the creature directly out my driver side window, it stopped sparkling because my lights weren't hitting it directly".

The hair reflecting his headlights when hitting the creature head on, then not reflecting as he drove by with only ambient light, indicates that the "sparkling" was not a self-generated or self-emitting event, just reflection.

So, in ending the most recent follow up, the two items shed no real additional light (no pun intended) other than the fact that my witness did not add another event or embellish anything from the original report. This is actually a good thing. It demonstrates that a good reliable witness who is both truthful and accurate would/could be someone to trust in future events. That in and of itself would be more valuable in the long run in the rare instance that he or she has another encounter in the future. This also further indicates that trained observers of the human condition and peripheral events are very valuable witnesses in this field. Law enforcement, military, airline pilots and similar safety-based fields are trained to observe and retain facts and data in a non-biased method. And this takes nothing away from any other witnesses by any stretch. Truth and honesty always win out. "Just the facts ma'am" as Jack Webb from Dragnet used to say. And if you remember that series, you're as old as I am.

10

BFRO REPORT # NA

Reprinted with Permission

Submitted by witness.

Possible sightings and strange incidents experienced over time on rural property.

YEAR: 2004-Present
SEASON: Fall
MONTH: November
DATE: 26
STATE: Arkansas
COUNTY: Private at owner's request
LOCATION DETAILS: Private at owner's request.
NEAREST TOWN: N/A

NEAREST ROAD: N/A

OBSERVED: We started hunting this 80 acres around 2003. I was sitting in my Deer stand when some dogs came barking through the woods like they were chasing something. They went up into this corner where the woods and the fence line meet and started rolling around in the dirt and barking so I got down to run the dogs off and to see what they was rolling on and when I got to the corner I could smell something that smelled like dead animal, musky and sour. Then as I turned something across the power line in the woods approximately fifty yards away let out this deep long growl. I have never heard anything like this in my life, so I started backing away and when I got to the path I ran to our truck.

After we got home my husband and I looked up growl sounds, and I never could find anything that sounded like this, and it was horrifying to me! I also had another incident with my husband back in about 2003 we was going out there to this property and feeding the deer. We were on our four wheeler and we drove to the power line and the man who owned the property had been there and bush hogged and had moved some tin that was laying there, and the grass was dead where the tin had been lying. Right in the middle was a cell phone so my husband picked it up and it had been chewed on by dogs or coyotes or something, so he laid it up on the tin which was about four feet away. So we filled our deer feeders and left. We come back the next day to visit the power line and the cell phone was back in the dead grass area exactly where we had first found it. So my husband picked it up put it back on the tin. So we check the feeders and left. We come back the next day drove back to the power line and the cell phone was gone and there in the dead grass area laid a piece of pipe about 2 foot long, so we picked up the pipe and put it on the tin and we left. We didn't get to come back the next day but the following day we came back drove to the power line and the pole was gone but there in the dead grass laid a little white button. It was the kind of button you see on mobile home ceilings. By this time we was freaking out. So we put the button on the tin, and I laid in the dead grass area a ponytail holder I had and also a mint. Nothing took the ponytail holder or mint. My husband found the cell phone again approximately seventy-five yards up the power line about a month later, but we never seen the pipe or the button again.

ALSO NOTICED: My brother-in-law was hunting by the creek and something big and black got up out of the creek and walked up the hill. He said it was on two legs and it was huge.

We purchased forty of the eighty acres two years ago and we were building our house and I found what appeared to be two tracks.

About twelve years ago just up the river from our land our nephew was fishing with his dad and saw a Bigfoot come down and scoop up water in his hand and get a drink. He said it was a blondish reddish color and very big.

OTHER WITNESSES: I was the only witness to the growl but my husband and I both witnessed the things being left in the powerline

OTHER STORIES: One of my friends approximately forty years ago was up on some old train tracks with her brother playing while her mother picked blackberries and she said that a big foot came up behind her and stood on the tracks. That location is approximately twenty miles East of our property.

TIME AND CONDITIONS: Late afternoon around 4:30 pm. It was sunny and kinda cool

ENVIRONMENT: It's all woods and it has a river to the west about a half a mile and several creeks

---

Follow-up investigation report by BFRO Investigator Carter Buschardt:

I have spoken with witness on several occasions. Although there are several incidents mentioned in her report over the years, I am going to focus on the gifting incidents, which are intriguing and not very often reported. I will include the other events at the end of my commentary, as they are of the more "typical" variety and do merit mentioning, and collectively they indicate an interesting series of events.

Back story is as follows: Her and her husband had been hunting the land since 2003, and they eventually bought it in 2015. They purchased forty of the eighty acres as mentioned.

The landowner had let them hunt the entire eighty acres previously, and also allowed them to place feeders to attract deer and other animals. They started placing feeders in different places and visiting the property more frequently after they purchased it, usually several times a week. The former landowner moved a stack of tin from an old torn down shed as he was helping them clear out some debris. Where he had moved the tin from, the grass was dead and they found an old flip phone.

They weren't sure how long it had been there, but it had chew marks on it, most likely from small animals. (Smaller teeth marks). Otherwise it looked like it might still work. They thought the owner of the phone might come looking for it, and they even thought the person they bought the land from had lost it, so they placed it on top of the remaining pile of tin. They left after filling feeders and came back the next day. The phone had been placed EXACTLY where they previously found it, right in the middle of the bare, flattened grass where they found it four feet away.

This was odd, and they weren't sure how or why it got there, but they put it back on top of the tin. They returned the next day and the phone was gone, and on the bare spot, in the nearly exact spot the phone had been, was a piece of plastic conduit about two feet long. It's getting a bit spooky for them, and since they had had previous events (and related tales of events with Sasquatch mentioned in the report), they began to wonder if this was somehow related.

They put the pipe back on the tin and returned the very next day, only to find the pipe was gone, and in its place was a small, decorative flower shaped button. They are used mostly in mobile homes to hide the nails on the ceilings. The nail is driven through a hole in the middle. She was familiar with these little buttons and was quite certain this was what it was.

So she left the button on the tin and placed a hair tie and a mint in the grass. (She had these items in her pocket). They returned the next day, and the button was gone but the hair tie and mint were still there. This entire series of events took place over about a seven to ten day period. As mentioned, they never saw the pipe or button again, but the husband did find the phone about a month or so later near the power line (clear cut) clearing. This was in the general area of her and husband's sighting of creature(s). The distance from the pile of tin to the bare spot was about 10 feet or so, so it is mostly unlikely that the phone, or other objects, slid ten feet off a two foot pile.

It needs to be mentioned that the former owner lived in Tennessee, and though there is a home there, no one lives or stays there. It is looked after by only her and her husband from time to time to keep it up and brush hog. It is very remote, and they have never seen anyone on the property, nor any signs it is being hunted or used in any way.

They, and or friends or relatives, have had other events, also mentioned in this report. One other event she did not include was a sighting by her husband in 2017 of two "dark creatures or objects" one taller than the other, also seen in the bigger power line clear cut at a pretty good distance. They were moving around, and his supposition was that one was sitting or squatting, which was his reasoning as to why one seemed taller than the other. It was just a "gut" feeling he had. There are two clear cuts, one big wide one for the main lines, and a smaller one to service the few homes around them. He also had a similar sighting three years prior, in 2014, but this was a solo creature about seven to eight feet tall.

The location is "in the boonies" and it would appear highly unlikely that anyone would go to the trouble of pranking them out in the middle of nowhere. The logistics and timing would be a miraculous series of events to pull it off. The witnesses had had a slight interest or knowledge of Sasquatch prior to 2003, and it has become more obvious to them as the years and events have gone by that it is most likely that they exist.

I do not doubt her story, as she was forthright and upfront in relating her accounts, and they did not waiver to the point that I ever doubted her credibility for a second. She and her husband were both spooked and excited at the same time regarding the events.

UPDATED 8/16/17: From the time I first interviewed the witness, and had written the above report, she has personally seen a large creature in the clear cut. This is the same clear cut her husband had seen one, and maybe two, creatures as well. She described it as having shoulders approximately three to five feet wide and was squatting down in the tall weeds, and the height of it from the waist up was approximately four to four and a half feet. She only saw from the waist up due to the tall weeds it was standing/squatting in. She was in a hurry when she saw it, as she was late for work, so there was no time for further observation or perhaps even a quick photo. When she came home, whatever she saw was no longer there.

Her husband had gone out on the property to get supplies together for food plots ready when he heard a "whoop". When he returned to his shop, he heard a single "knock", from the area near the food plots he had just returned from. I mention these events as peripheral incidents to support the ongoing activity on the property. They have shared many photos of maps of the areas for the gifting incident, as well as the sightings. As mentioned before, though there have been numerous other incidents; growls, whoop calls, structures, sightings of solo and multiple creatures, I am concentrating solely on the gifting, as it indicates an unusual interaction that defies a rational explanation.

UPDATED 11-22-17. Since the report was originally published, they have had sightings of one and two creatures on several occasions. They are usually, but not always, in the clear cut shown in the photos, but at a good distance away, about a quarter mile, and usually as she is leaving for work. One was standing and the other crouching or kneeling during one sighting. Another sighting had one walking until they looked at its direction, then it froze. The exact spot they were seen in were different each time, and there was nothing there when they returned.

They do have bear there, but being avid hunters, they are absolutely certain they are not bears, both by upright movement and general stature.

Updated June 2021

This report was originally going to be in this book from the start but circumstances on their property started heating up about the time I was putting things together and I decided to hold off. It appeared at that time that they were heading towards a habituation situation, and at the very least a visitation situation. Though I have mentioned elsewhere in this book, to redefine (as I see it) the difference between the two classifications, a **visitation** is mostly a coexistence where neither party really encourages nor discourages any type of interaction. No feeding or gifting with rare exception. Just a glimpse or a knock or call here and there without returning the favor.

Habituation is an overt act by the property owners to encourage activity either by feeding them on a somewhat regular schedule, and or gifting them food or trinkets. If one hears a call or knock you return the act. Or you begin the act and hope for the Sasquatch to return the favor. One has to really want to interact with them and I always tell my experiencers to be careful what you wish for. And that is what I told my folks here. They are somewhere in between the two classifications with some random food gifting and encouragement in other ways. On the fence so to speak. So when she called me on June 23, 2021, in an excited panic, I was not totally surprised. This will be the third update in writing since I first spoke to them in 2017 when they filed their original report. She was outside laying on the deck by the pool just sunning herself mid-afternoon. These are her words exactly. "This past Monday I was in my swimming pool and had been cleaning it. I was taking my net and scooping up the trash then I would hit it on the metal part of the pool to knock the trash out. Then I started noticing a whistle. It was just a short whistle, and it was coming from the woods across the power line. Then a few minutes later it was on the woods on our property.

I got done cleaning and was laying on my mat and I looked and saw a reddish brown something looking around some bushes. It looked like part of a head and a shoulder. I kept watching it and it didn't move so I thought I would float over to get a drink and go back and see if it was there. When I floated back it was gone. Then a bit later I heard the whistle in the woods behind the house. Later that evening after Hubby got home we was sitting outside and heard a perfect wood knock in the woods left of our house. We also heard another wood knock Wednesday evening coming from same area.

Thursday I was back in the pool. I always take my 9 mm out with me. I keep it in a little tote by the pool. I don't keep one in the chamber because I carry it in my purse. I got in the pool and always have to clean out the leaves/bugs and I heard what sounded similar to a buck grunt. I kept cleaning and heard it again.

Then a bit later I heard a limb break. It was kinda windy, so I thought maybe just the wind, but I went on ahead and kicked a shell in my chamber. Hubby has a bunch of metal down the wood line where we heard the knocks. Well, a bit later I heard what sounded like metal hitting metal. I was getting a little spooked by then. I started getting stuff ready to get out and I always take the net around and get out any more leaves/bugs that fell in and as I was cleaning, and I looked up and about forty yards away I saw something standing there. Our yard is twenty yards and the driveway was about twenty yards from the woods. I could see the head, torso, arms, and most of the legs. I saw the hair hanging off the arms. I couldn't see face details because the hair was over the face. I looked at it for about three-seconds and looked back down. I was afraid that if it knew I saw it that it might come closer. I took a few steps forward and the roof of the carport blocked my view but then I thought I have to look back so I took a few steps back and it was gone. That made me doubt myself even though I saw so much detail. Hubby looked for a sign. He couldn't find anything. That made me doubt myself even more. But I know what I saw. I could see the reddish brown hair hanging down off the right arm. The sun was hitting the right side. It was so clear and so real.

Hubby said when he was looking that he was leaving indentations in the leaves. So I don't know. Maybe it was further back. I had Hubby stand where I thought it was and it was a good foot taller than him. He is 5-11. And the shoulders was a lot wider and the legs much longer and bigger. All I know is I've seen this twice and Hubby and I both heard the wood knocks, and I heard the grunting and the metal hitting metal. I debated on whether to tell you because we couldn't find any sign, but I know what I saw. Idk where it went, and it must have been super-fast. Or it could have just hunkered down... idk I'm puzzled and doubting myself even though I know what I saw. I thought you might find this interesting. And btw I heard you on Bigfoot Odyssey. Hubby and I like watching and listening to that. Very interesting stories".

Follow Up Conversation with Both Witnesses.

Several points come to mind and in no particular order of importance here they are. First, when she saw the Sasquatch it was a full frontal view, clear as day. She saw the long wings of hair hanging from its arms and sides. The reddish brown hair was also cascading over its face and eyes. The sun was glistening off the hair and in no way shape or form was it anything other than a Sasquatch, period as it stood seven to seven and a half feet tall. In my honest opinion this being wanted her to see it. It was an intentional exposure. They have seen numerous others, and probably this one as well since they bought the home in 2015. They have seen most or all of them from twenty to forty yards away to several hundred yards to a quarter mile up in the two clear cuts on their property. There have been numerous events of knocking, some gifting back and forth, mysterious photos on trail cameras, knocks, calls and whistling. Little twigs, and rocks tossed at her while she has been in her blind. I could go on, but I won't. You get the drift. Their files are crammed full of samples of nearly everything you would want to validate they have something very special and unique going on there. These beings have been living on this virtually vacant land for generations perhaps. Long before they came along in 2015. They are willing to share the land.

Secondly, when she saw the creature, its hair was hanging down over its face and eyes. She described it as clean looking and well kept. Even the hair hanging down from the arms was clean and distinct. A few hours after the event she began to wonder if it had covered its face because it was seeing a woman in a bathing suit and it was somewhat shy or embarrassed. She never saw the eyes and I think she was disappointed. The being did not look like she thought it would look like. I hear that often. Many have the preconceived notion of the grimacing snarling and growling beast of the woods so often portrayed in artwork, film, media and marketing ploys.

Most encounters are not of the threatening variety. Some probably are. But where does the fear really emanate from? From us humans who have the mindset that they are vicious creatures waiting to rip us to shreds via the media prototypes? Yes an eight hundred pound Sasquatch who is seven to ten feet tall and built like a linebacker can be intimidating. I cannot say I would not take an extra breath if one suddenly showed itself. Human nature.

Another thing she mentioned was when she looked at it, she heard a voice in her head say, "don't look at it". Was it her voice, her inner voice that we all have that tells or warns us to do or not do certain things? Or was it the Sasquatch telling her not to look at me? That has been reported as well. Many that mention the voice in the head will tell you they heard "don't look at me" versus "don't look at it". Don't look at me insinuates it comes from the Sasquatch as it is referring to itself in the first person. Don't look at it insinuates it could be your inner voice warning you. Any hunter will tell you not to make eye contact with certain creatures in the woods, as that is taken as a sign of aggression or threat.

All in all I estimate at a minimum they have seen Sasquatch at least a dozen times in total or partial sightings. Everything from an arm or leg to the most recent full body exposure. Multiple sightings in the clear cut to a blurry something blowing by them in the woods or peeking from behind a tree, all at various distances.

Toss in the knocks, whistles, twig snaps, and little things being tossed at or near them. There have been a few gifting experiences with some marginal success other than the original gifting of the flip phone which was the catalyst for the original report. For me that is a classic example of give and take with a being that does not "exist". Since they have hunted this property since 2003 and owned it since 2015, there were many times they thought they heard or saw "something" but chalked it up to the usual and customary random fill in the blank explanation many experiencers come up with. Add in the half dozen or so neighbors and or family members within a twenty mile radius that have and are having experiences as I write this. It is a secret club of sorts. As it is in small rural areas where everyone knows everyone, and they know at least some of your personal business, you have to pick and choose whom you tell what. It is self-preservation. There are no secret handshakes or passwords to join the club but some reading this will understand the stigmas associated with seeing or experiencing seriously out of the ordinary beings that we are taught/told do not exist.

They have a decision to make as to whether they want to encourage the activity and interactions or keep it as it is at a distance.

They can no longer deny or explain away anything any longer. It is a real and palpable experience they are having. Encouraging a habituation relationship has its positive and negative positions and needs to be carefully thought out. I cover that extensively in Chapter 11.

As her hubby pointed out in our last conversation, "I kind of like them at a distance right now". It may stay that way for now and just see how this new relationship goes. The ball is in their court, and I of course wish them the best either way it goes for them.

Great shot of one of two power line clear cuts on their property. Phone was found in the middle of the patch of daylight and placed on metal for former owner to find. It was moved back to patch of daylight, then it disappeared. It was found months later halfway up the clear cut right in between wood lines. It didn't blow up there.

11

VISITATION & HABITUATION
REAL LIFE AND CURRENTLY ONGOING

Visitation and Habituation

    This chapter I will go over three of my current four visitation and habituation witnesses and describe the difference between visitation and habituation. There are a few subtle and not so subtle differences. These are <u>my</u> descriptions (definitions) and may or may not be similar to anyone else's. Doesn't matter really, almost one and the same.

VISITATION IS ALLOWING the creatures to come and go with no encouragement or discouragement. A great example of this are my witnesses who have a farm with twenty plus acres. The list of events going on for nearly a decade are numerous. I have taken good solid prints there (see photos near end of chapter). They had three confirmed sightings, one really incredible one. Many sightings of "bushes" that were not there the day before and are gone the day after sighting. These are seen a quarter mile away in pasture, and they have seen them moving and stopping when the "bush" knows it's been spotted. People riding horses have seen them move, leaving the horses visibly upset. Fifty pound bags of dog food pulled through a small locked doggy door, bag and all. An eight to nine foot tall Sasquatch carrying a dead deer over its neck and around the shoulders, backlit at just the right time by a bolt of lightning, witness was thirty-five feet away. A scene right out of a horror flick. The usual howls and knocks. Possible mane braiding, though the jury is still out on that one. They have a peaceful coexistence to the point they forget things to tell me when we are catching up. Went to the grocery store, got the car tuned up and oh yeah, saw or heard a Sasquatch Thursday.

My point is the witnesses here do nothing to encourage the visits, nor do they do anything to thwart the Sasquatch visits. This is visitation. Come and go as you please, just put the toilet seat down as a courtesy for the wife.

They were at first unnerved at the original sightings but were at the same time enthralled. After we met and spoke and discussed Sasquatch behavior (as we perceive it to be on the day of this writing), they were much more relaxed and open to it being a real thing. Yes, it's a thing. There are times they see them, times they hear them and times they sense them. Sometimes they will go for a while with no activity at all. At least as far as they know. They are perfectly happy with this arrangement. They want them just where they are and there is no desire for any direct interaction. They do feel privileged to have them on their property. We did discuss habitation & they wanted no part of it. They had youngsters at the time.

HABITUATION is a LOT of work in the end. That is why many are content with visitation. If one really wants to get to know Sasquatch up close (potentially), it is possible under very, very unique situations, but it does happen. But it's not for everybody. Be careful what you wish for. Habituation is generally providing water, shelter and or food, especially foods they don't get in the wild. As with many creatures, including us, they will get used to the routine and get a little grumpy sometimes when an expected meal, or other treat, is forgotten. Habituation is also encouraging events and or interactions any way they can. This too can become problematic. Again, be careful what you wish for.

Another witness couple entered into a short-lived habituation situation and have let it devolve into a visitation which continues to this day (2020). When they first contacted me about four years ago, they were having stick and branch breaks, bi pedal movement in the woods, a few structures near a deer feeder, huffs, howls and very low grunts and growls. These grunts and growls were putting their very large dog, one hundred and twenty pounds., on high alert. Hair standing on end, and growling. This dog fears nothing, and she would not go into those woods under any circumstances when this occurred, and in fact, she would sometimes cower and want to go back in the house.

She had no problem running into the woods when she heard deer or small critters, but this was entirely different. She would also go on alert while in the house and sometimes growl with her hair standing up and other times whimper and cower in the corner.

Since they were experiencing this on a regular basis, and by doing a little online research they deduced it sounded like possible Sasquatch activity and contacted me through my web site I had at the time. We met, chatted and after that they seemed mostly at ease with what was going on. Since they were encouraging wildlife activity by having the deer feeder, they were generally just enjoying watching whatever wildlife passed through. They do not hunt.

The husband did more research on the subject and we discussed the possibility of putting out food for them away from the feeder and trying to get some shots from a trail cam.

Sounded good to me. Even though there is a pretty well-established aversion to cameras by Sasquatch, it's always worth a shot. Only takes one slip up to get a money shot. They had been in the habit of taking leftovers outside after dinner and tossing them near the woods where the feeder was. We decided to try a spot near their barn where there was a flat fence rail attached to the side of the barn. It was about chest high. I explained that placing food here would make it available to virtually any forest animal that wanted it but that is where they wanted it. All good, and yes, we got the usual and customary suspects feeding there. Raccoon, possum, mice, hawks, etc. All caught on camera. The camera was strapped to a tree about twenty feet away, and it was mostly hidden by a stack of old barn wood and some brush. Twice there was food taken and no camera shot. The camera had caught nothing, but the food was gone. It was working fine, as there were photos taken the days before and after. Weird but not unheard of. There were several days when none of the food was taken. Everyone was probably full.

Long story made short we removed the camera. After that the food routinely disappeared, paper plate and all. No plates were ever found whole or in part anywhere on the property.

They always took the food out on a paper plate and when there were very few leftovers, they had two small rocks they used to weigh the plates down so they would not blow away. Months went by with this scenario in place. Since this setup seemed to be working, I decided to expand the venture by replacing the food with a jar of peanut butter. This has been tried often with varying levels of success.

Remember, Sasquatch love human food, especially the kind they virtually never see in the wild. Sweet moist peanut butter is one item, as well as candy bars and bananas. We put the jar on the fence rail and the lid was hand tightened as tight as it would go. The hope was getting fingerprints if we were lucky enough to have the jar opened on the spot. The jar just sat there for a few days, then it vanished. We looked everywhere for it and it was gone. About two weeks later my witness found the jar and lid in the woods. We had missed it somehow I suppose. Maybe not. Conjecture here. The jar had been almost cleaned out, and since it was exposed to rain and the elements, it was dusted and there were no prints to be had. I tossed it back out where we found it, as there was still some yummy peanut butter in the bottom. And yes, there are other animals that can open jars like that. Check the internet and there are plenty of videos of raccoons, foxes and other animals rolling a tightly screwed on lid up against trees and rocks to eventually loosen the lid. Actually, that act in and of itself is a quite fascinating stand alone event to see.

Well, not to be outsmarted again, this time I tried another jar and super glued the lid on. I was pretty sure it would take a figurative blow torch to get it open. It was placed on the fence rail (see photos) and sat there for about a week, then it was gone. Before it disappeared, he took a photo of it after he had gone out to check on it. He called me totally blown away by what he saw. Remember the 2 rocks they used to weigh down the paper plates for the food offerings? Well, there were now THREE ROCKS AND THEY WERE STACKED ON TOP OF ONE ANOTHER. This was an overt act of communication!

Now during all the feedings, and the peanut butter experiments, they were still experiencing the sounds and visual events (movement in the woods, snapping branches, structures and arches etc.). That new super glued jar eventually disappeared as well, and it was never found. So, they had a nice little habituation going and it was running on all cylinders, but it was getting exhausting for them. Day after day of feeding them and other than the peanut butter rock stacking, there was not anything captured on cameras since it was deemed counterproductive. That was by agreed upon choice by both parties with no regrets. Without a doubt the rock stacking was an awesome event and was an act of communication by a thinking sentient creature. But they decided to take a break from the regular feedings and just go back to the tossing of leftovers out in the woods as before.

This is where it gets good if it wasn't already. Their daily routine was the husband getting up around 3AM daily to get ready for his hour drive into the city for work. The wife got up shortly before he left to do her get ready for work routine as well. After about two weeks of no feedings, and after hubby had left for work, she began seeing shadows pass by her bathroom window. It was a typical opaque glass block window that allowed light in but did not offer a clear view of anything. It was placed above the tub and was at least seven feet off the floor. This happened a few times and of course the dog went apeshit. Pun somewhat intended.

Then the banging on the outside of the home started. On several occasions she grabbed her pistol and the dog and out the door they went only to find nothing.

Now the shadow and banging happened on one or two occasions when hubby was home, but it was primarily when he was gone, and she was home alone in the wee hours. And the banging happened almost always on the bathroom side of the home, which was also closer to the woods. And coincidentally or not, she was the one who had been taking the food out to the fence rail for the majority of the time. And I don't believe in coincidences anyway. It seemed to be targeting the person who was doing most of the feeding. So, they were getting grumpy about the discontinued feedings and they were letting them know about it. Habituation gone awry, perhaps. Be careful what you wish for.

So, it was decided to try to catch them or it, in the act. And yes, another trail camera attempt. They had a large stack of firewood placed between two trees in the front yard. At least a cords worth and probably more. Stacked about chest high a no more than twenty-five to thirty feet from the front door.

Easy access when it was time for a short run to get more wood and it faced the part of the home where most of the shadows and house slapping occurred. I removed about eighteen inches of wood in the middle of the stack and placed my camera there and stacked the wood. Pretty clever I thought, though I was certain they were probably watching me the whole time. Camera was facing the side of the house as well as the front. Well, nothing for about a week, then some sporadic banging on the opposite side of the home hidden from the camera. Then another pause which lasted a few days. Then one day they called me to tell me all the firewood had been removed all the way down to where my camera was.

Two feet of stacked wood had been knocked off the stack, leaving my camera just sitting there on top like a chimney on a rooftop. If that wasn't a message, then I don't know what is. It was not at all subtle. Boom! Take that smarty pants researcher! Message received loud and clear. And no, the wood could not have fallen or rolled off from the sides. Remember, it was stacked nice and tight between two trees.

That was about two years ago, and we have since abandoned the camera traps, and the banging and shadows eventually ceased, as did the regular feedings. I guess the Sasquatch got their message as well.

There were other peripheral events going on during the cessation of the feeding. There was an old baby buggy that had been tossed far back in the woods no telling how many dozens of years ago. It was there when he bought the place. It was the older kind with the small chrome tube frame and frail wheels from the 60's or 70's. It was actually partially buried in the dirt it had been there so long. It suddenly appeared in the middle of a well-worn game trail they often used for hikes one day, and it was close to the deer feeder.

Very odd and who the heck would do that anyway? Very random. It is very private property with dozens of fenced acres. Perhaps a form of gifting from the Sasquatch? Here is a little gift so please bring us food? Conjecture, but not out of the question by any stretch. Actually, I think it more likely than not given the overall situation. Oh, and the first jar of peanut butter that we found mostly eaten and tossed back in the woods? I was later found by my witness tightly wedged in the fork of a tree about seven feet up. Totally cleaned out.

The witness was reflecting back with me one day and he mentioned that he had bought the house a few years before he met his wife. He made an offer to the owner and it was a bit of a low offer and he assumed the owner would counter back.

It was listed "as is" and though it was inferred that there was nothing wrong with the home, he made a lower offer in case there were hidden issues. The owner accepted the offer on the spot. No haggling. He had the home inspected, and it came back clean as a whistle. When he again contacted the owner to settle on a close date, the guy informed him he had already moved out of the home shortly after inspections and move in whenever you want. Awesome news. He was there five days later to move his stuff in.

When he unlocked the front door all the guys possessions were still there. Furniture, pots, pans, refrigerator with food still in it. <u>Everything</u> except clothing computer and TV's. And I do mean everything. Tools, mowers and items in the barn and shop. He called the guy to see if he had somehow mistaken the move in date, and the former owner said, "keep everything, sell it, burn it, give it away, I don't care. I'm never going back to that home" Then he hung up.

My witness later found out through the small town gossip grapevine that the previous owner had complained to a few folks that, "there was some weird stuff going on out there, and I'm selling the place". It was never mentioned what the weird stuff was, but he was good to his word and he sold it. I still see and speak to the witness and his wife to this day. And there is still peaceful activity. I have reviewed well over 30,000 photos from this property alone. Sometimes tiring, but it really never gets old.

This is activity with my third and final habituation witness. The fourth witnesses I mentioned at the beginning of this chapter have literally just begun their journey into the visitation and it may evolve into a habituation relationship. Baby steps. Maybe another cool story for another time.

This witness and her family moved to their isolated and beautiful property about twenty years ago. I have been there, and it IS a little slice of heaven. Back in the very early nineties, either '91 or '92 she had a sighting of an eight foot tall reddish brown creature as she was driving home one night. When the headlights hit it, the creature threw its arms up to cover its face. It was massive and at least six hundred to eight hundred pounds. This event was never reported publicly, and it is only mentioned to assure the readers that she is familiar with Sasquatch.

Fast forward to present day. They have had activity for most of the nineteen years they have lived on the property, sometimes sporadic and sometimes fairly regular. Since there has been a lot of activity up to the point where they have been encouraging further activity, I will just point out certain events in abbreviated form to get the readers up to speed.

Keep in mind these are just few of the numerous events they are, and have, experienced. I just want to let you see that it is one long and ongoing journey for them, and it continues.

1. When they first moved in, they were hearing all kinds of screams, violent sounding shrieks, whoops, whistles and what she self-described as the Ohio moan howls. She looked it up on the internet. They chalked all this up initially as forest sounds they just weren't familiar with yet. Sound familiar?
2. They had moved her mother and her mobile home onto the property so they could take care of her in her senior years. Once she was moved in, her mother told her that things were hitting the trailer at night and she could hear heavy walking around outside as well. It was also throwing rocks against the outside of the trailer and tossing rocks on the roof as well. Then it began throwing rocks at the witness' home as well, and on the roof and porch also. **Someone** was obviously not happy with the new living arrangements.
3. Her mother was picking up the rocks in the yard that had been thrown at the house before the yard was mowed. On two occasions, the rocks were thrown back near her on two separate days. She never saw who or what threw the rocks. This also happened to my witness several times when she would be weeding her mom's yard.
4. They had two dogs on the property and every now and then a pack of wild dogs would come by their property,

and other neighbors as well, and harass the dogs by barking and snarling at them as wild dogs will do. Her mom came out one night to run the dogs off and she heard clear as day something "firmly and loudly talking towards the pack in a very loud animal language" she had never heard before or since the incident. The dogs turned and left. Her mother added that, "if an 800 lb. gorilla could speak, that would be the sound".

5. When one of their dogs died, my witness' husband buried the dog in the front yard of her mother's trailer. On the one year anniversary of the dogs passing, they planted fresh flowers all around the grave as a memorial. The next morning when they went outside, they discovered that all of the flowers had gently been removed from the grave and gently laid next to the hole they were in. No damage to the flowers in any way. She asked me if a Sasquatch would do that and I could only offer "conjecture" as to why a Sasquatch would not be fond of a marked grave. I told her I believe they bury their dead when possible. And, a marked Sasquatch grave is a good way for a human to find a body.

6. Her husband worked nearly two hour drive from home one way. Nearly a four hour round trip. She and her daughter were home alone during nearly all the events. He got home, heard the latest tale and pretty much said yes dear. Then he went to bed. This went on for years. He believed SHE believed something was out there, but since he was rarely there, he could only nod and say okay. Now he did hear the occasional howl, knock or scream, but that was about it.

So, this will get you mostly up to speed up until he retired and spent all his time at home with the usual and customary foray to town for domestic needs. From this point on I will be outlining his indoctrination into the events his wife had endured for years and years.

Remember there were weekly, if not numerous days in a row, where there was either subtle or overt activity. Though those are important, the individual incidents are simply too numerous to catalogue here. Some were significant, some were pedestrian as far as Sasquatch events go.

(This was about the time the witness first contacted me.)

So, her husband began hearing the sounds with far more regularity and clarity since one of his new retirement duties was to walk the dog in the morning. He would traditionally walk him to the front gate of the property and back, which was about a quarter mile or less from their home as I recall. It was usually early in the morning just at or after sunrise. He also got the sense of being watched and heard something paralleling him in the woods as he walked the dog. Not every day, but often. Slow bipedal steps that were sometimes heavy, sometimes soft, but they were there. He was slowly starting to get the picture.

Another day he was going to start working on their truck at the barn at the bottom part of their property. When he pulled in down there, he saw a "giant something" that was neither man nor bear. It ran away so fast he just could not say what it was, but he knew what it wasn't. Shortly after that he started finding footprints down there. And other places as well on their one hundred and twenty acres. More pieces of the picture were coming into focus. Perhaps his wife was on to something. An apology may soon be forthcoming.

Next is her hubby's aha moment. This is the wife speaking, "So, at the end of last summer I bought a cheap little night vision scope. One night I asked my husband if he wanted to go out and sit on the front porch with me. He said ok, so we went outside and turned on the scope and started focusing it on the woods across the road from our house until I had the right distance. This was where there had been a lot of activity over the years. As I had it focused and was scanning the woods, to my utter amazement there it was, fifty yards in front of our house where I had seen them before". (Don't get me started on coincidences, you cannot win). "As I was looking at this creature, I screamed out, "Oh my God, dear, it's bigfoot!" I was certain he was thinking yeah, right. But I handed him the scope and pointed at where to look and said it's standing right there. I waited a minute and asked do you see it?

He said YES, I see it! I said I told you there was a BIGFOOT, and it was out there! And here is her description of the Sasquatch:

> "This thing was standing there watching us as we were watching it. It was at least eight feet tall or even taller and huge. Its arms hung down past its knees and kind of curved like a monkey's would. Its head was crowned to some degree. We passed the scope back and forth. My husband couldn't believe what he was seeing. I watched it crouch down then stand right back up.
>
> While we were watching that one, another one threw a rock onto our carport. (Maybe it was ducking while another one threw the rock?) My big brave husband wanted to walk out to it. I told him it could rip him apart with little effort if it felt threatened. As he started to walk out towards it, there was a sudden flash in the scope, and it was gone". Her husband had just been baptized.

The witness called me a few days later. We had had a long conversation when we first spoke, and she outlined all the activity on her original report. We discussed me visiting their property sometime, and she said anytime. I hopped on that offer like a bargain bin shopper. I ended up spending a full day and night at their property. Very warm, generous and kind folks. I was there within two weeks.

On the day of my arrival, they drove me all over their property. One hundred and twenty acres is a lot of ground to cover, but I got the best guided tour ever.

There were obvious nesting sites, a few structures, tree snaps at the appropriate height for a large strong creature. We visited the site where her mom's trailer had been. And the dogs grave still had a little marker on it. Their home is smack dab in the middle of Mark Twain National Forest, so their property has the exact terrain, food & water sources need to support a large alpha predator group or family unit. Could not design it any better myself.

We sat down at the kitchen table and had a great conversation regarding all the activity from their report, and all the activity that was too numerous to mention. Plus, the items mentioned on the previous pages in this report.

The wife had seen a group of at least three and she felt like it was a family unit. There were not clear as day sightings, but creatures moving through the brush and trees in the daylight, giving glimpses that left something to be desired, yet she knew what they were. There were shadows and silhouettes of giant and juvenile humanoid shapes moving through the woods at dusk and again, she knew what they were. She even mentioned that when she would be outside doing chores and singing out loud, there would be activity in the form of a knock, whistle, or something moving around.

There had been many footprints, and actually, as I was writing this book, they sent me photos of four more prints they found in January 2020. And as luck would have it, I had left them several pounds of Ultracal casting material when I left. They used every bit of it. As we spoke further it was clear there was a lot of activity going on there and experienced by the entire family over a fifteen to twenty year period. I had no doubt as to the sincerity of the family. A devout Christian family who wanted nothing more than to share their stories and get some reassurance that was no danger in having them around. We discussed taking the presence of the Sasquatch to a different level which would of course be a habituation situation, and I mentioned gifting as an easy entry level activity. They were all on board with it. They began gifting bags of apples and in return, small rocks started turning up in the front garden next to their home. Sometimes groups of rocks, sometimes just one. The rocks could not arrive there randomly, as her hubby keeps a meticulous yard and garden.

The yard looks like it could be on a golf course. That part of the home is forty yards or so from the road in front of their home, and it is a chipped rock and dirt road anyway. A rock(s) would have to be thrown or carried there. (which has been done numerous times before remember?) The gifting is random and not regular, on both ends, but it is a start.

I did sit on the porch with them at night for a few hours with our night vision and thermal equipment and it was a great time, expounding on theories and past experiences. We focused on the woods directly across from the front of their home, where the majority of activity seemed to come from. Other than a few interesting sounds and thermal hits that were partially blocked by woods, or too far for any possible identification, there was nothing profound. But the company was awesome.

When it was time to crash, I parked my Jeep across the street on the previous site of her mom's trailer. I slept in my vehicle. Other than a few twigs snaps and rustling in the brush, there was no research grade activity.

In the morning before I left, I went to the woods across from the house and placed five hand mirrors in various trees as an experiment. As I approached the woods there was an obvious heavy bipedal crashing in the heavy brush about 30 yards away as my best estimate. Five steps then silence. My sense was the steps were not trailing away but getting closer to perhaps observe what the heck I was doing in "their" woods. These were the woods where much of their activity had come from, include the movement of humanoid shapes. Yes, it did startle me and yes, I had that being watched feeling that is so often reported. I walked on in further to where I was originally headed.

I had picked the spot the day before and knew where I wanted to place the mirrors. I hung my mirrors in five different trees, all within sight of each other. I would say within a thirty to forty foot area. Yes, there was that feeling of being watched the entire time. It wasn't because I was initially startled, but it lingered because I was almost certain I was within twenty-five yards or so of one of these creatures.

Can't prove it other than my years in the woods and that innate human characteristic of just knowing when something is off. My experience, and thus, my reality. We **ALL** have that sixth sense. For some it is more pronounced and slaps you in the face, and others it barely registers. I then went to their home and had a great breakfast and final conversation, then hit the road. I have an open invitation and will back.

Habituation and visitation witnesses.

These types of witnesses and ANY witnesses really, need to be treated with dignity and respect, <u>especially</u> if you are a researcher. When any person has an event such as a face to face daytime encounter, or a nighttime of growls, bluff charges, rock throwing and or walking through their camp, whether awake or asleep, or just pick an event, they are often initially seriously shaken. The fear of shaming and ridicule by friends and family is a real thing. These responses just keep otherwise excellent witnesses from coming forward at all. These ongoing habituation/visitation events need to be slowly nurtured and encouraged. And if the witnesses decide they have had enough, so be it. Doesn't matter the reason. Treat them as you would want to be treated.

And remember this. If you, as an investigator, show up dripping with electronics gear and the activity ceases, don't be surprised. In fact, even a visit from <u>anyone</u> outside the family known to live there by the Sasquatch can stop activity. They get used to the cozy little existence. Stranger danger.

Photos from habituation witnesses

CARTER BUSCHARDT

You can see the toe impressions are obviously there. They cast it, and ran out of plaster before I could get there to help finish it. The print is nineteen inches long and a tad over eight inches across the top. That is a big fella right there. Mid tarsal break is clearly there. Print is hanging in my office.

They did a good job overall in making the cast. The ruler is there for referencing the inch to inch and a half depth of the print. The soil has a lot of sand in it, as it was at the edge of a pond.

SASQUATCH

Peanut butter container stuck in tree

THE FIRST JAR of peanut butter after we had found it opened and mostly emptied. After we knew there were no prints available from exposure to the elements, we just tossed it back where we found it since there were still a couple of spoonful's left in it. It was found jammed in the fork of this tree not far from where we found it.

Nice act of gifting, or just messing with us. There were two of the rocks the witnesses used to weigh down the paper plates already on the rail. A third was added and the rocks were stacked. Note the geometry. Largest on bottom for strong foundation and smallest (capstone) on top to finish it off. This takes thinking and logic. It may seem insignificant but it's not at all. They did not take the bait. Also takes thinking and logic. Small things.

One of numerous footprint photos sent to me. The print is 14 inches long and 2 inches deep. They had been taking photos like this with no frame of reference as to size. They now send with objects placed nearby some of the time.

Remember, there is such a regular amount of activity that it just isn't all that important to them at the time. Like seeing deer tracks. Yep, there's another one dear. Size was determined by later measuring the husband's boot which was shorter than the print.

Two fingerprints found on the saddlebag of a motorcycle stored in the barn. Bike is rarely ridden and may not even be running. The amount of dust would indicate it's just been sitting. They do hear sounds every now and then of someone rummaging around in there at night.

Since we discussed moving on with the habituation, they have allowed me to experiment with the placement of mirrors in the woods, directly across the road from the front of the home. This is where they get a good bit of activity.

If you search the internet for reactions of animals to their reflection, especially apes, chimps, orangutans, etc., it is quite interesting. Some are quite amusing, and some react with hostility and frustration. Imagine seeing your clear reflection for the very first time.

Mirrors hanging in the trees

Other than a reflection in a body of water or a random view if you saw yourself in a vehicle or home window, a clear view of one's self for the first time would maybe be a seminal moment for these Sasquatch.

My original intent was twofold. I was hoping to get a fingerprint from the handling of the mirrors by a curious Sasquatch. It would have had to happen fairly quickly after placement, since a print will degrade with exposure to the elements. And it would also require my witnesses to check the mirrors with regularity. That's a lot to ask.

The other intent was to perhaps get a vocal reaction from a Sasquatch to the discovery of the mirrors, in the rare hope that my witnesses would happen to be outside and hear the discovery/reaction at the very moment of discovery. That is also a lot to wish for, but one never knows. The best scenario would be for one or more of the mirrors to just disappear. Since the mirrors were hung with heavier gauge picture frame wire the odds of them just falling off are not great. Possible but not great.

My witnesses did decide to move the mirrors further into the woods after seeing some of the angry reactions on the internet of the animals seeing their reflections for the first time. The odds of them taking it out on my witnesses is minute but better safe than regretful. As I told them, I was pretty sure I was being watched when I put them up and would be just as certain that they would be observed when moving them. But I am also just as certain that curiosity will get the best of them. Too tempting to just leave them be, especially if you catch a glimpse of yourself for the very first time. Another silly human hanging stuff in their living room.

I have sat on the front porch of their home with my witnesses at night and just listened and watched. There is an area across the gravel road where the Sasquatch will occasionally gather, and they seem to know when they are on the porch. They do have occasional interactions. On one night we traded calls back and forth. We also have traded rock clacks and twig/branch snaps back and forth. It is an awesome event. I highly recommend it.

12
QUANTUM PHYSICS / PARANORMAL / ABSTRACT CONCEPTS

Artwork by Sybilla Irwin

"I think, therefore I am". - Rene' Descartes

This chapter is going to deal with many theories, conjectures and concepts regarding Sasquatch behavior and or skillsets. Some of these will include the observations of witnesses as it pertains to either a clear sighting of a Sasquatch and or an encounter where the Sasquatch was heard, or presence was felt but not clearly seen. Basically, Class A or Class B events as defined previously. The sightings will also include things that are not the run of the mill sightings. Yes, this will include events best described using quantum theories and abstract theories as potential explanations, since they will fall outside the usual Sasquatch events.

Many of the other concepts and theories put forth will be from other sources, such as published books from very well respected authors in our field, experienced investigators and researchers whom I know and respect personally, and some witnesses whose events were not outlined in detail here, but have valuable insight simply because something unique happened to them that lays outside the "normal" boundaries of reported sightings.

Normal here means yours, or a witnesses' perception of an event that was seen and or experienced by them. It happened unmistakably and without question. It is their reality. Rejection, ridicule, scorn and other typical human reactions will most likely not dissuade them from believing what they saw.

It can, however, dissuade them from talking about it to anyone that they otherwise thought they could trust. It is denialism at its finest. Look it up. I'm no shrink but denialism is a thing. A very real thing.

> **Denialism.** In the psychology of human behavior, denialism is a person's choice to deny reality as a way to avoid a psychologically uncomfortable truth.

But all I ask is that you at least consider and read with an open mind. I'm NOT asking you to believe any of the theories. Just read, absorb, consider and do what you want with it.

We deny and or outright ridicule (or worse), things we do not understand or WANT to understand. It is an unfortunate part of the human construct. **Traditional science** is one of the greatest offenders. Since we simple humans look to traditional science to answer many of the questions we have regarding the mysteries of our universe, planet and lives, most of us will take what they say as gospel and go on with our lives. If the government, traditional science, and other sources of revered information tell us it is or isn't so, so be it.

> "There are no unnatural or supernatural phenomenon, only very large gaps in our knowledge of what is natural... we should strive to fill those gaps of ignorance". Dr. Edgar Mitchell / Astronaut. Courtesy of Ron Morehead.

But in defense of **traditional science, they are not equipped to handle the esoteric and abstract theories presented by some of the witnesses.** Yet we have been turning to them to explain things in a three-dimensional way when a much more complex explanation is possibly needed, especially when it is a complex witness event. It's like trying to work on a Porsche engine with a flat head screwdriver and wire cutters.

So, I am going to delve into quantum science to explain what more and more witnesses are reporting. For quantum science, some of these concepts and theories are discussed as possible and maybe even probable. Remember, theoretical but possible. Same **theoretical** discussions as flight, computers, planetary exploration, robotic surgery and nanotechnology.

Those subjects, and countless others, are no longer theory. The Star Trek and Einsteinian world is upon us.

> "A theory in Classical Science is established by repeatable experiments and then it's accepted by academia. It's based on everything being physical or material, measurable and predictable. A theory in Quantum Science is considered differently. If the subject was

established by mathematics, in order to disprove it, it must be disproven mathematically". Quote courtesy of Ron Morehead.

If a witness reports orbs, portals, cloaking, multiple dimensions, infra sound, etc., then it is a responsibility as a researcher/investigator to at least consider it. Same goes for the casual and curious readers.

Hmmm, interesting concept but I'm not sure I buy into all that paranormal stuff.

That's fine, I'm just tossing it out there. Just like Brussel sprouts. They're on the plate, but you don't have to eat them. Just an option.

And I also ask you to consider this fact. And it is now a FACT. The U.S. government has admitted that UFOs are real. They don't say they are piloted or controlled by intelligent beings from another planet. Not just yet anyway. Many of us know better. But they have to spoon feed us slowly as they secretly remove the egg from their face. But think back a few decades to our current day. Remember the outright denial by the government that UFOs were real. They embarked upon a campaign of misinformation, sidestepping and in many cases, public ridicule. Swamp gas and birds reflecting lights off their bellies, among other garbage theories and explanations. I remember them well. I grew up with it. Witnesses, otherwise sane and rational people, were ostracized and ridiculed. NOW, they are vindicated. UFOs are real and a thing.

Fast forward to today. Apply the last paragraph on the previous page to Sasquatch and it's a mirror image, except traditional science and the government are still at the denial game. Walls built with lies and denial used for mortar, will always come down. Just a matter of time. We need to let traditional science off the hook a bit here. They are ill equipped to handle much of this abstract subject matter.

(One final thought and I'll get off my soapbox.)

Treat witnesses with the dignity and respect you would want. It might just be you one day. If your spouse, parent, child or very close friend were to share an abstract happening with you, what would you say? To their face? We are taught what to think by those who do not necessarily have our best interests at heart.

Some of this will blow your fricking minds. There, I said it. Remember the Brussel sprouts. A healthy option. They won't kill you. At the very least you may have broadened your horizons. If nothing else, spread them around your plate so it looks like you ate a few, just like when you were a kid. You may have fooled your mother, but only kidded yourself. Read this chapter with an open mind is all I ask. It'll be our secret.

Think Einsteinian, Hawking, Planck and yes maybe even Star Trek. And of course, Brussel sprouts.

THE FOLLOWING excerpts are from reports that you will not find on the internet. They were told to me and or other researchers/investigators via face to face, emails and or phone conversations. First you will read the portions of the reports that mention or relate to the potential abstract, paranormal or quantum explanations as they were sent to me. Could be a paragraph, could be a sentence or two. Then where possible, I will have followed up with the witness after the original transcript was sent.

THIS FOLLOW up is both with investigator and or witness permission.
And obviously the identities and specific locations, if private property, will not be used. These are real events.

> *The opinions I offer here do not reflect those of BFRO in whole or in part. I cannot speak for them or any other investigators, groups or researchers with any other groups unless they have agreed to be quoted here. The opinions are mine and mine alone.

Also keep in mind, that by considering these events as told to me by a witness, it does not mean I believe them right off the bat. I take into consideration the demeanor and veracity of the witness as it pertains to everything else they describe. If an otherwise sane, rational and lucid person reveals an event that not only matches up with other unrelated witnesses across the country, but also begs an outside the box, quantum or technical explanation, then they will get the respect and obligation due to them as an investigator. We owe them that much. They may just be on to something.

Illinois 2014 or 2015. This author and a half dozen or so seasoned investigators were on night ops in some heavy woods in southern Illinois. We were call blasting whale, dolphin, and other calls into the woods. One of our party stayed behind in his vehicle to blast the sounds into the woods, and we were monitoring the woods for any responses or activity. Within thirty minutes we got a panicked call from our guy in the van. He needed us back right away, and we ran, as good as one can run in pitch dark, with gear strapped to you.

We got back and he told us he clearly heard a car pull up behind him (no lights), gravel crunching under the tires, car shifted into park, engine turned off and car door slammed shut.

He fully expected someone to walk up to the car (a curious game warden or sheriff came to mind). But they drove up dark, no headlights. And if a warden or sheriff suspected poaching or another crime, it IS possible they would pull up with no lights.

But even if so, the sounds of the car were unmistakable and there was nobody there. Though it was cold outside his driver's window was down so he could blast. He heard everything clearly and with no doubt as to what he heard. This researcher was a degreed scientist with a pedigree most would envy, and his word was always golden. He was not a guy that would even consider pranking or hoaxing. That was something that was not even in his wheelhouse.

Author synopsis: A perfect example of mimicry & perhaps infra sound. Perhaps a form of hypnosis.

1970s. This is an excerpt from Ron Morehead's book, *Voices in the Wilderness,* 2nd Edition. Copyright©. All rights reserved. Page 29. Reprinted with permission.

> "We were about 15 feet apart as we began slowly creeping up the ridge. My eyes were opened as wide they could get, and I wasn't about to blink. Surely this creature had to be behind one of those giant cedars. After walking about 30 feet and exactly at the same time, we both froze in our tracks, unable to move forward.
>
> "We were just a few feet from a huge cedar when we looked at each other. "I don't know about you but, I can't go any farther-we need to go back" Warren said. I agreed. This paralyzing effect was not explainable, and it wasn't fear. It may sound crazy, but it seemed like we were being blocked by a force field, like in the old Star Trek episodes".

He brought this event up to a scientist a few years later who believed in the possibility of the Sasquatch phenomenon, and in a nutshell, he suggested the possibility of pheromones or maybe infra-sound. Hypnosis maybe?

Iowa 2011 or 2012. I (this author) was on a small private expedition in Iowa and two of us had pitched our tents in a wide-open field used primarily for campers with horses and trailers and it was closed for the season. It gave us a wide open view of the surrounding forest for nighttime thermal viewing. I awoke one morning right as the sun was coming up to the sound of footsteps approaching, and since I needed to relieve myself anyway I thought I'd get up..

Since I assumed it was my fellow camper, though the footsteps were coming from the opposite direction, I thought I'd go ahead and check. I lay there for a few seconds to fully wake up, and the footsteps got closer and heavier. Very heavy. I tried to move in my sleeping bag but just couldn't. As the steps were probably 25 feet away (estimation) they were thunderous. Not human and not my buddy. I was fully awake, no sleep paralysis or dreaming. Just wanted to get up and relieve myself and see what was out there. But I couldn't.

Yes, it was cold outside, but not that cold. The need to stay warm was overridden by the need to pee. I heard and felt the ground shaking steps as they were right next to my tent and headed towards where I knew my buddy was camped, about 100 feet or less from my tent. Once the steps faded to silence, I was able to get up.

Once outside my tent I took care of business. Then I saw my buddy exiting his tent to do the same thing. It wasn't him. He just got up. I thought it was odd at the time and just thought I was being lazy, but I just couldn't get my arms and hands to unzip my bag.

Author synopsis: Infrasound or hypnosis.

IN 2015, I interviewed a man who with his boss, observed a large Bigfoot walking through a forest. Right before it was going to exit into a large plowed field, it walked "behind" a tree and never emerged the other side. They went down to investigate to find there was no way it could have escaped their line of sight. They we're baffled as I was, at the time...

Interviewer Name withheld.

Author synopsis: Vanished right before their eyes. Portal or dimensional event?

OR: *"If they are interdimensional the Sasquatch converted to 'energy only' and went inside the tree"*. This Quote courtesy of <u>Ron Morehead</u>

December 2016. Family driving through a very large forest when the driver sees a Sasquatch standing in the middle of the road on a hill. Driver assumes (after we discussed the event) that the creature is using the high spot on the road as a vantage point to see traffic coming from both directions. It was 5pm with plenty of light.

As it turned to walk into the forest it "appeared to be a **distortion in our reality**, and then it just disappeared". Witness also stated "I have a background in quantum mathematics and share the strong belief that these entities are inter dimensional". Calculations indicate that this type of event is mathematically possible.

Author synopsis: This appears to be an example of dematerialization.

"Mass to energy and back again." Quote courtesy of Ron Morehead

---

Florida 1977. Follow up conversation with witness by this author. A 12 yr.. old (at the time) boy was doing one of his weekly chores by taking garbage out before the school bus came to pick him up. Sun was already up. He went out the front door and headed to the back yard where the trash cans were. (No back door, they lived in a trailer). He saw a "huge creature bent over one of the trash cans eating scraps". It was no further than 60 ft. away. Upright creature on two legs, covered in long reddish- brown hair. It was massive and about 8ft. tall. He described it as more manlike than animal. When he rounded the corner of the trailer, the creature saw him and just froze, as did the witness. Their eyes were locked for what seemed like an eternity. The event was actually more in the 30 second range. As they stared into each other's eyes, he heard very clearly, a voice in his head **that was not his inner 12 year old voice,** that said **"You (man) are not of this world (planet).** At 12 years of age, he had no knowledge or even a concept of "mind speak and or voices in his head" and only a very minimal general knowledge of Sasquatch. I will say this changed the course of his life to this day. Another subject for another time. But this guy's intelligence factor is way up there. We spoke for an hour. He has both found answers and discovered new questions. A journey in progress.

Author synopsis: An example of mind-speak or mental telepathy.

———

August 2001. Excerpts from an interview with a Sasquatch sighting. Witness sees a Sasquatch cross the road in front of their car. Broad daylight, around 10AM. The witness heard very clearly in her head **"I just want to be left alone".** This just blew her mind. The creature looked her way briefly then continued across the road. It knew she was there. As she drove on less than a half mile, she noticed six SWAT team cars parked on the side of the road she was on. She pulled over out of curiosity and approached the only officer she could see. She asked him if there were officers out in the woods and he replied there were. She then said, well I just saw something cross the road (without being specific) and the officer just stared at her, turned around and walked away without saying a word.

As she drove off, she knew in her heart they were hunting for this creature. Whether it was thinking "out loud" or actually speaking to her specifically, we will never know. Did it need or want her help?

Author synopsis: Another classic example of mind-speak or mental telepathy.

———

SASQUATCH

EVENT OF 2004. Witness was at his apartment around 11 pm with a couple of his friends. They decided to go down to a heavily wooded creek behind his apartment. This was an area he fished at, and in the past, he had experienced some "weirdness". A strange "whump" sound, which he described as sounding like dynamite blasting in the distance. And it was more like he "felt it than heard it".

He also had pebbles or small rocks thrown at his feet as he fished. There was a nearly full moon, so they easily got down to the creek and were just enjoying the babbling creek, chatting and smoking.

After a few moments they heard the same "whump" off in the distance, and they were "feeling the sound waves as well as hearing it". Small rocks were being tossed at them as well. The forest life went silent. The sound got closer and closer and they all panicked, and they began to get the heck out of there. They all "felt the force of the sound".

As they ran up a hill back to his apartment, they had to stop to catch their breath. They were huddled together in a tight circle. The sound "got right in the middle of them and the force of the sound (whump) pushed them all backwards".

They decided to start running again, uphill, towards his apartment, "totally freaked out". One of the guys stopped running, since he was just tired of running uphill, and he reached down and grabbed a rock to throw at whatever it was that was chasing them.

A "black shape or force appeared right in front of him, and he froze on the spot, arm cocked back to throw with rock in hand". One of the other guys grabbed him and "snapped (shook) him out of whatever trance he was in". "He was frozen solid".

Once he came to, they finished their climb up the hill. At the top of the hill, there was a small field between them and the apartment, and it was somewhat lit up from the parking lot lights. As they were still running, they turned around to see if whatever was there was still coming after them. They all saw two large black shadows "following but not really chasing them".

The shadows were lit up by the parking lot lights and were clearly there and moving slowly.

Author synopsis: This event appears to be an example of perhaps two things, infra sound and cloaking.

*****

"Once at the Sierra Camp, while a creature was vocalizing just outside our log shelter, feeling bold, Warren Johnson and I, decided to rapidly go through the opening and get a glance at what was making those sounds…thinking, of course, it would run away. As we slowly walked toward where we'd been hearing the sounds, and without talking to each other, we both were froze in our tracks. In my book I describe it as likening to a force field in Star Trek. The late Dr. Leroy Fish said it was probably one of two things, Infrasound or Pheromones. Infrasound is used by many large animals. Pheromones are effective within the same species.

That said, I used to think that it had to be Infrasound, however, now that some genetic DNA studies have showed them to be part human, it makes me wonder".

Quote courtesy of Ron Morehead from his book *Quantum Bigfoot*. All rights reserved©.

EVENT 1970's. This is another excerpt from Ron Morehead's book, *Voices in the Wilderness,* 2nd Edition. Copyright©. All rights reserved. Page 30-31. Reprinted with permission.

"There was also another very unusual type of sound we experienced one night. After bedding down, we heard crashing, rowdy metallic sounds. It sounded like our ringed barrels, where we stored our food, were rolling down towards the creek.

These barrels were bound to the trees with cables, and to rip them from the trees would have demanded a bulldozer. But when we gazed out of the shelter, we noticed that they had not been moved-not even a little. Nothing had been disturbed. And we didn't see anything that could have caused those sounds". These sounds were heard by multiple witnesses and they really had only two choices. "We all, collectively thought we heard those sounds, or we did hear those sounds".

Author synopsis: Nearly identical to the event on a previous page. Infrasound, mimicry or perhaps mass hypnosis.

YES, these events happened, at least in the lives of the experiencers. Incredible as they may seem. And there are hundreds and hundreds of these type events reported yearly. And if the supposition that we only hear about 10-20% of all reported Sasquatch sightings is accurate, then think about what we aren't hearing. Many will report a "standard" Sasquatch event, if there is actually such a thing as a "standard" sasquatch event. Then at the end of the interview, they will say "I know you won't believe this but". Then they will throw in a quantum/paranormal event. Of course, you're relating your sighting of a Sasquatch to me, which is incredible enough on its own. And for the finale, you inform me the creature just vanished before your eyes, or whatever other incredible event you witnessed. Many of these type reports are just sent to scrap heaps by researchers.

The standard reaction of most of traditional science and many researchers is that, well, we can't get anyone to believe us as it is, I'm not going to throw the "woo factor" in there. They'll laugh us off the farm.

My position is that, since they (traditional science and a good part of the public) are laughing at us, and mostly ignoring us anyway, why **NOT** consider the esoteric and paranormal? What do we have to lose? Virtually nothing I say. Certainly, no respect will be lost, because we (researchers) and witnesses are getting virtually none anyway.

Many of the greatest achievements in medicine, technology, exploration etc. were discovered because someone took the extra step (chance) no one else would take. What is any different with this subject? Yes, these are flesh and blood creatures, but it is possible they may have other incredible attributes/skills that are discarded at a wholesale level.

If you don't **know** virtually everything about a subject, then as a researcher or scientist, or even the casual reader, you should at least **consider** virtually anything that comes into view. Any good researcher, reader or scientist, should have an open mind. How else do we learn? Brussel sprouts.

And if you do open your minds, then it will be our little secret. I will say nothing. Promise. What happens in quantum physics stays in quantum physics.

Who are they? What are they doing here? Are they one of us? Are we one of them? Have we assigned them quantum skills because that explains witness hallucinations? Or, do they actually have quantum attributes and we are just looking at it all wrong? Are we just clueless? Arrogant? Why no bodies? Do they bury their dead? Do they "go somewhere else" to die?

> "An effective researcher does not selectively search for reports that fit his or her paradigm. None of us actually know, so a good researcher must keep an open mind. We search and research for the Truth, and that Truth will defend itself"
>
> Ron Morehead's quote from his book *Quantum Bigfoot*. (I could not have said it any better).

Final Thoughts, Musings and Recipes

Well, there you have it. I poked the bear and spoke of the

elephants in the room in the previous chapter. Kind of like crossing a busy street of knowledge. It's hard to dodge **ALL** the cars when you're playing in the middle of the road. But I like the risk. Keeps things interesting, and in realistic perspective. If you're standing on the curb or sidewalk, watching all the abstract and quantum cars go by, well it's safe. And if you need to cross the busy street you can get to the crosswalk and push the button. The roaring stream of esoteric cars will part so you can safely cross unscathed.

And there is not a darn thing wrong with keeping your life safe, predictable and virtually uncomplicated. There are many days I daydream about just that. There is a lot to be said for order and simplicity. I am certain I would have aged slower and better if I had gone that route. If the topic of Sasquatch is just of casual interest and it sounds like a good subject to grab a book on for some mental stimulation or entertainment, then by all means go for it. Perfect subject.

But if there is a serious interest in this subject, or **ANY** subject that requires outside the box thinking then go there and go there often. If you like the world we live in now with all the major advances and comforts in whatever field that may include, then in each and every field someone took a chance. They thought outside the box.

They considered the abstract, quantum, outside the box theories because they weren't getting answers in the traditional way, traditional science included. And yes, whether you like the world we are in or not, scientists, researchers, inventors, etc., took chances. And here we are.

But in the scheme of things, research into the existence of this being needs to step up. We are slowly creating a body of evidence with mountains of reports from the very pedestrian to the very complex sightings. Massive footprints, some with dermal ridges. Structures, rock stacking, howls, knocks, etc. Blah blah blah. All been covered here and in countless other books. They are indirectly/inadvertently calling out to us, but we keep hitting the ignore button.

If we have seemingly (obviously) hit a dead end with traditional science, why not give the quantum end of it a shot? What is there to lose other than your membership in the Everyone Else is Doing it Club? It can still be your little secret. The Sasquatch beings can't possibly exist, and on top of that, do some of the crazy things that the crazy people report. They just appeared and disappeared right in front of me. Nothing can do that. Well, except an octopus or chameleon to name two. But not a Sasquatch?

And that physical transformation we see is the manipulation of chromatophores that carry different pigments. Take that physiological skillset to a quantum level for a possible explanation. Remember, I said possible, not probable.

What am I doing mixing a cephalopod with a reptile? Paying a visit to the island of Dr. Moreau? Nope. (I just dated myself). Just consider that these beings can somehow manipulate their surroundings and or their physiology. Maybe it's a physical transformation or something on a quantum level. A combination? Is it a form of hypnosis or infrasound? And this is just one of the skillsets reported more and more by otherwise sane respectable people.

We accept that some creatures can do some incredible things because we can see them do it right before our eyes. And we can see them in a video or in a zoo. (another subject for another time). AND "science" gives us their blessing.

Imagine being the first human to see a chameleon change and trying to explain it to a disbelieving someone. "Sure thing Bob, and we'll all have whatever he's having". We can all hear the eyerolls. We are still applying old school 19th century science to state of the art events. Old Bob is probably laughing in his grave.

It is a very complex subject, the quantum aspect. And this old hippie only has so many brain cells left to dedicate to understanding. Times a wasting as they say. If the traditional scientific community is failing us, then let's step off the sidewalk and at least try to cross the street. We can always hit the crosswalk button if we dare go no further. Einstein, Hawking, Plank, Ramanajuan and others can't be all wrong.

Myself, I cannot look a witness in the eye and tell them they are imagining things when they tell me things they see and hear that are outside the "usual and customary" Sasquatch event. Why? Simple. I do not KNOW those things cannot or are not happening. Chameleons and Octopi. Nor can I look at myself in the mirror if I were to ever blow off a witness because they told me something extraordinary and quantum like.

When you hear it in their voice and or see it in their eyes, that all they want is for someone to listen and receive the information and want nothing in return, then do it. You may be helping them in ways you can't imagine. Yes, some of the things I hear make very good sense in a quantum way. Other things I hear I continue to research and learn. It is not an overnight process. I'm still learning. And you? Open or closed for business? Consider it if you will and discard if you must.

And that recipe I mentioned? I just discovered after sixty plus years on the planet that you can cook bacon in the oven faster and cleaner than the old pan fry method. It honestly never occurred to me to look at cooking bacon differently. And you know what tastes even better? Simmering those infamous Brussel sprouts in that awesome bacon grease. What a treat! Another new adventure for this old hippie. And I am actually going to eat all my Brussel sprouts. Not going to fool myself, or my momma, or anyone else, by spreading those sprouts around the plate.

We all need some expansive thinking.

13

HANDPRINT, STRUCTURES AND OTHER RANDOM PHOTOS

Pyramid Credit: Nina-No/Nina Aldin Thune©. Tipi (Teepee) Credit by John C.H. Grabill©. Sasquatch structure photo. Carter Buschardt©.

Does it make you wonder? It Should.

Some of these photos are related to other events already mentioned in this book. I will refer to the event and page number when possible.

Fellow BFRO investigator Shawn McLeran at Welcome Arch
Michigan 2016. He is 6ft. 1 inch tall. Arch was at least 7.5ft. tall.
Soaking in the vibes.

SASQUATCH

Caroline Curtis, Shawn McCleran & Jim Sherman
BFRO

Brian Woods & Shawn McCleran.

IN APRIL OF 2016, fellow BFRO investigator Brian Woods cast a handprint in a research area we have been working for numerous years. The below photo he took after casting it using Ultracal casting material. As you can see, the site was about one hundred and fifty to two hundred yards from the road we use to get there.

The assessment of the location was that the creature was kneeling with the bush as a bit of cover facing the road. (arrow) Hand placement was used to brace itself in the very moist mud. The final print had excellent dermal ridges. Handprint was nearly thirteen inches from base of palm to tip of middle finger. Photo before we dusted it with fingerprint dusting powder. Congrats to Brian for finding this!

Photo of left hand. The NBA called me, looking for this guy.

Print after dusting. Left hand.

SASQUATCH

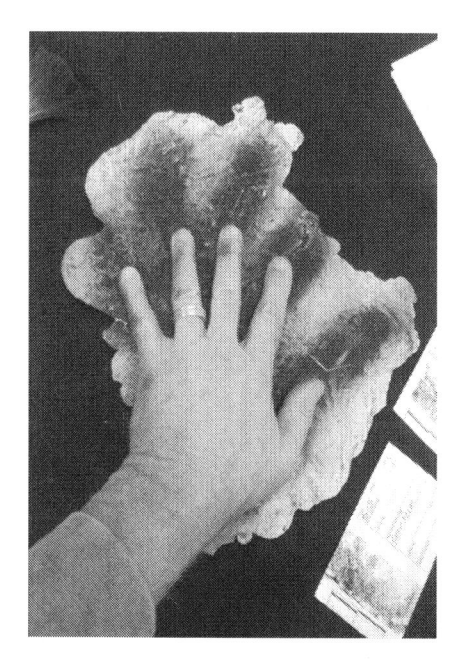

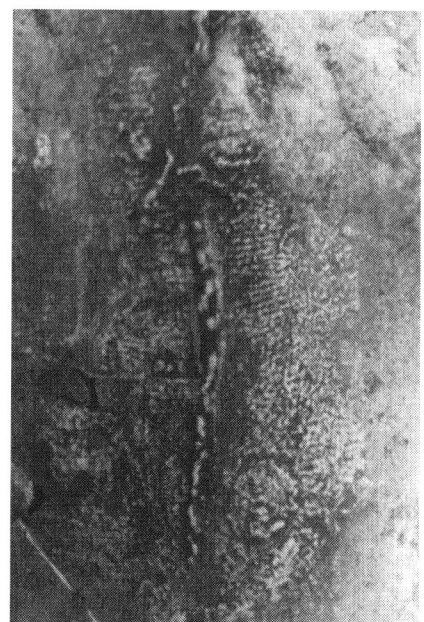

Very clear and unmistakable dermal ridges.

Print cards.

We did the traditional dust and lift and transferred the prints to the print cards. By the way, if you are a researcher, **you should always carry a DNA kit and casting material** with you at all times. This is an obvious reason why.

Here is the clincher. Through connections, these prints were sent to a forensics lab. Not Uncle Bob's mail order lab set up in a garage. A state-of-the-art Criminal/DNA/Biologic Analytics Lab. They were confirmed as genuine unaltered untampered prints. They were not faked. The person doing the testing also indicated they did not want to know who or what made these prints. Just a little spooked. Since the prints went into this lab, they **had** to be run through the nationwide criminal database. Results: the person who made these prints had no criminal history. Good thing. If they only knew.

SASQUATCH

Native American glyph we found in Illinois

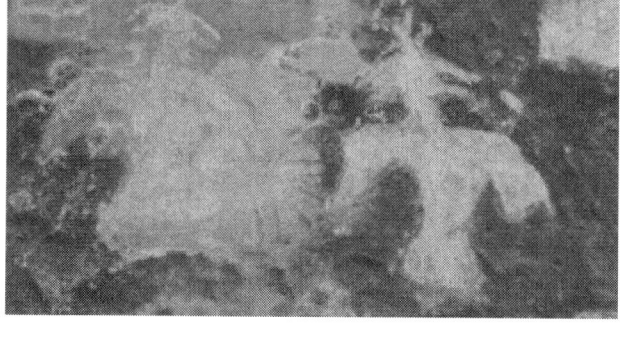

Random tree falls? I think not.

Close up from above photo.

Epic example of Native American trail marker tree, which was added onto by Sasquatch, or "persons unknown". Pay close attention to area highlighted by arrow on left in next photo. Illinois 2013

The top of this tree was driven deep into the ground and other smaller sticks have been added over the years. Remember, they are talking to each other. What the heck are they saying? Same tree Illinois 2013.

What can I say? Impressive as heck. Native Americans and Sasquatch still have a symbiotic relationship that has withstood the test of time. Illinois 2013

Not to be left out, trail marker tree in Missouri. Below is another angle.

To MAKE these two photos perhaps a bit more interesting, myself and two others had a Class A sighting, at night, through a thermal camera. Two of the three of us were sitting with our backs to these trees, unbeknownst to us at the time. When we went back the next morning to recreate the event to get distance measurements, we found these.

This is in an active research area and this has been a reported travel pathway for Sasquatch over the years. I have had two Class A reports published to BFRO within a few miles of this location. Very wide creek bed with a large sand and rock bar in the middle. A perfect watering hole for major Sasquatch food sources.

And every now and then we got a surprise visitor at the research area base camp. We had just put a pan of gourmet sasquatch goulash on the fire and an interested black bear came by for a bowl. Rain check issued.

Open Minds, Open Many Doors

The End.....For Now.

AFTERWORD

So Now What?

So, after writing this book, my very first, it appears to be time for reflection on what left my brain and landed on paper. Sort of like sitting back after a big meal and thinking I actually enjoyed that. Maybe less fried shrimp and more salad and veggies. More or less of one or the other. Eat the same and exercise more? I'll dwell on all that. It is strange yet exhilarating to see your thoughts dimensionally. Everyone should try it at least once, just like skydiving. Take a leap of faith, literally, open the chute and enjoy the ride. I was going to say, "what's the worst that could happen" but you are already thinking I'm not jumping out of a perfectly good plane. But I did and I'm still here, ruptured eardrum and all.

First and foremost, I am a researcher. I absolutely love speaking to witnesses in the field or on the phone. I love absorbing their events and passion about what they experienced. Only then do you realize they are sharing an intimate and sometimes life changing moment with a perfect stranger. These are moments reserved for only the people that are very close to them. Why tell a perfect stranger, who would be more likely to reject them than just about anyone?

AFTERWORD

Trust

They trust the investigative process. Just listen, discuss and collect all the data. No smirking or wisecracks. Big word for just 5 letters. Just look them in the eye, or listen intently, and gather it all in. No judgement. Judgement on the spot is not in your job description. Certainly not in mine. As a researcher, you are certainly aware of the number one reason people don't talk about a Sasquatch event. Ridicule. Fear of ridicule from everyone from spouses, co-workers, friends and family, etc. That fear will shut them up faster than a witness in a mob hit trial.

No matter the details of the event, from a road crossing to the very intricate, complex and abstract, we need the open and understanding minds of everyone.

If we silence one mind by overt ridicule and judgement, then we silence at **least** ten more without even knowing it. Think or say that out loud. Do it again.

I will say this once more, mercifully for you the reader, since it is the last swing of the bat in this book, that if we don't know everything about ANY GIVEN subject, then we need to consider almost anything, however abstract, until we get to the bottom of it. It is easier to reject things outright because it doesn't fit our paradigm and it's less work. Where would we be today if that's all we ever did?

And that is where we go out on a limb and perhaps try a different version of science. One that can at least absorb and postulate on a very specific point(s). As I mentioned in the Science chapter, we have simply been posing the questions we have about Sasquatch to the wrong branch of science. They simply can't, or won't, give us any help.

We have been banging our heads against the same wall for the last fifty years!

This is where quantum science could likely be of some very big help. It is more likely quantum research could confirm or deny many, if not all the theories the public has regarding these beings, and many other non-Sasquatch subjects as well. As with most things in life, physics and biology pretty much answer most any questions we have about life.

>**Physics**: the branch of science concerned with the nature and properties of matter and energy. The subject matter of physics, distinguished from that of chemistry and biology, includes mechanics, heat, light and other radiation, sound, electricity, magnetism, and the structure of atoms. **Definition courtesy of Oxford Dictionary**

>**Biology**: the study of living organisms, divided into many specialized fields that cover their morphology, physiology, anatomy, behavior, origin, and distribution. **Definition also courtesy of Oxford Dictionary.**

Boy, that definition of physics seems pretty far out there. Almost science fiction huh? Almost sounds like that dirty "Q" word. If you open your mind just for a few moments, it will be our little secret. Promise.

>According to 19th century German philosopher Arthur Schopenhauer, "All truth passes through three stages: First, it is ridiculed. Second, it is violently opposed. Third, it is accepted as self-evident."

My second book in my series is available.

Sasquatch: Evidence of an Enigma II

ABOUT THE AUTHOR

Carter Buschardt is an experienced outdoorsman who has been researching Sasquatch for over two decades to include eleven years as an investigator with BFRO and is trained to be an investigator for MUFON as well. His extensive work with BFRO includes interviewing over three hundred witnesses, resulting in nearly one hundred published reports to the BFRO web site. He's a true, boots on the ground researcher / investigator who has met and visited the properties of nearly half of the witnesses whose reports have been published.

While his knowledge of Sasquatch is vast, his special interest in the creatures focuses on long term habituation sites, burial research, infrasound, language and stick structures. Not a desktop warrior, he stays active in field research and actively monitors and visits several properties with ongoing habituation activity to this day.

He's a native of Texas and currently lives in Missouri.

Printed in Great Britain
by Amazon